What the
**Science
of Reading
Says**
about

Word Recognition

Jennifer Jump, M.A., and Robin D. Johnson, Ed.D.

Other Books in This Series

Contributing Author

Alan Becker
Greenville, North Carolina

Contributors

Dani Battle
Former Second Grade Teacher, Baltimore, Maryland
Tyisha Brown
First Grade Teacher, Naperville, Illinois

Publishing Credits

Corinne Burton, M.A.Ed., *Publisher*
Aubrie Nielsen, M.S.Ed., *EVP of Content Development*
Emily R. Smith, M.A.Ed., *SVP of Content Development*
Véronique Bos, *VP of Creative*
Cathy Hernandez, *Senior Content Manager*
Hillary Wolfe, *Developmental Editor*
Jill Malcolm, *Graphic Designer*
David Slayton, *Assistant Editor*

Image Credits: p.75 Tada Images/Shutterstock; p.84 Ben Molyneux/Shutterstock; all other images from Shutterstock and/or iStock

A division of Teacher Created Materials
5482 Argosy Avenue
Huntington Beach, CA 92649-1039
www.tcmpub.com/shell-education
ISBN 978-1-0876-9669-0
© 2023 Shell Educational Publishing, Inc.

Table of Contents

Introduction

Welcome from Jen Jump

The Hippocratic oath is powerful. Most of us have heard it spoken of, usually in passing, perhaps while watching a medical drama on television. We often think of the oath in terms of the simple phrase "Do no harm." The reality is that the oath is much more substantive. The language is intense, lofty, and powerful. According to tradition, medical professionals have been swearing some form of the Hippocratic oath since the fourth century BCE. Without parsing out the implications and utility of the oath to modern-day medicine, most people know its purpose and relevance.

The current version of the oath (revised in 1964) articulates several thoughtful tenets that stand out:

1. **I will respect the hard-won scientific gains of those physicians in whose steps I walk, and gladly share such knowledge as is mine with those who are to follow.**

   Yes! I want every doctor I meet to listen to the knowledge gained from the physicians who went before them. I want my medical professionals to share what they learn from diagnosing and treating me. In the same way, I want that for my educator friends. I want us all to remember that the successes and failures of the educators who have gone before us, the hard research studies undertaken, and the seminal understandings gained pave the way for us. Many scholars have shown us the way over the years, with the goal of ensuring that we use these bodies of knowledge and understanding to provide the best for our students.

2. **I will remember that there is art to medicine as well as science, and that warmth, sympathy, and understanding may outweigh the surgeon's knife or the chemist's drug.**

While medicine is largely clinical (the science), there is an art to it that includes listening, considering, and understanding. Realizing there is an art to teaching creates the possibility of joy and passion, along with challenge and precision. It is the art, when matched with the science in education, that ensures that students are considered first. It ensures that families and caregivers are seen as partners and that the classroom is a dynamic place for all.

3. **I will not be ashamed to say, "I know not," nor will I fail to call in my colleagues when the skills of another are needed for a patient's recovery.**

It is my hope that a doctor, when stymied by a condition or illness, will be open to the support of a colleague, optimally one who has researched the condition or has a deeper understanding based on experience. Educators, too, should strive for the candor of asking for help and for the willingness to listen. As professionals, each time we open a professional resource, read a research article, or engage in professional learning, we are acknowledging that there is more to know.

In essence, the oath speaks to us, as educators. We can align our professionalism to that of medical professionals. We, too, consistently promise to "do no harm." We create classrooms filled with joy and learning, love and laughter, and rigor and challenge. While there is no formal oath for teachers, each day upon beginning class, we promise to listen to the wisdom of the research, to remember the art and science of the work we do, and to be unafraid of requesting help when needed. We are dedicated.

It is not always easy. Sometimes, the research is complex, confusing, or seems contradictory. Education can be a whirlwind. Standards change. Curriculum changes. Expectations change. Legislation changes. And lately, these changes are compounded by added pressures. But, the need for young people to develop literacy skills does not waiver. Reading, writing, speaking, and listening consistently reign as must-have skills.

Several years ago, I stood on a stage in front of eager educators, ready to begin the new year. We were talking about literacy, engaged in the conversation around the importance of reading challenging texts. Education was in the midst of change, and for many, it was an intense, scary change. The research (what we now call "the science") was indicating the need for systemic change. We needed then, as educators need now, to be ready, willing, and able to heed the research and orchestrate instructional change within our classrooms. The purpose of this book is to support that goal.

What Is the Science of Reading?

This book is one in a series of professional resources that provides a close look at the discussion around the Science of Reading (SOR). What exactly does that mean? The term the *Science of Reading* pervades the national conversation around the best literacy instruction for all students. The purpose of this series is to close the gap between the knowledge and understanding of what students need to become literate humans and the instructional practices in our schools. This gap is widely acknowledged yet remains largely intact. While research is available, journals are not easy to navigate. "It would be the proverbial needle in a haystack problem trying to find the most relevant information" (Kilpatrick 2015, 6). With concise resources that build understanding of the body of research, however, teachers can be equipped with the logical steps to find success. Mark Seidenberg notes, "A look at the basic science suggests specific ways to promote reading success" (2017, 9).

> We create classrooms filled with joy and learning, love and laughter, and rigor and challenge.

The great news is that this book will help you navigate the important research that informs the Science of Reading conversations. Let's begin by quickly breaking down the words behind the hype: the *Science of Reading*.

> **Science:** a branch of knowledge or study dealing with a body of facts or truths systematically arranged and showing the operation of general laws or systematic knowledge of the physical or material world gained through observation and experimentation

> **Read[ing]:** looking at carefully so as to understand the meaning of (something written, printed, etc.) (Dictionary.com 2022)

Bottom line? The Science of Reading is the collection of excellent research that leads to the understanding of how students learn to read. What are the best ways to support students as they break down the code of the English language? How can teachers provide the best instruction for developing fluency? What are the structures within text and embedded within instruction that will best support students as they decipher text and develop the skills to understand a range of genres in various contexts and content areas? Which strategies will best help students develop the ability to write with adequate voice, grammatical control, and knowledge? The answers are found in the collection of research, studies, and experiences (the ultimate educators of the universe) known as the Science of Reading. Many of the research studies have been duplicated, reinforcing the understanding of how students learn to read.

To be clear, nothing about this body of work is brand new. There are ebbs and flows within any conversation, and while some of the conversations around the SOR have resurfaced in recent times with great enthusiasm and debate, the basic components of this body of research have been discussed among literacy researchers and educators for many years.

Figure I.1—Components of Literacy

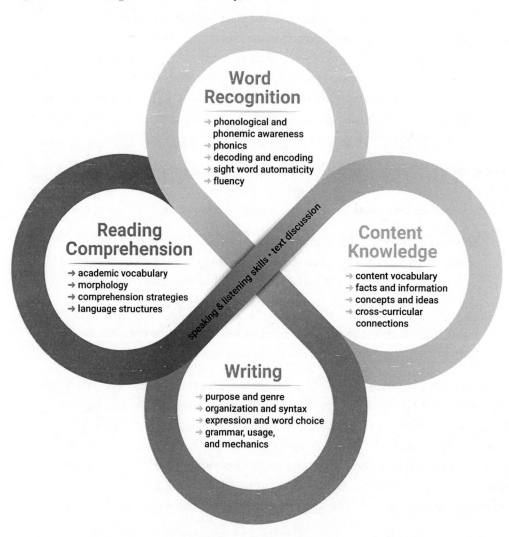

Figure I.1 demonstrates an approach to linking the research-based components of the Science of Reading, highlighting word recognition, reading comprehension, content knowledge, and writing. A very intentional decision has been made to include the science of *literacies*, including reading and writing as well as recognizing the power of speaking and listening, in this series. Each book will explore instructional implications, best practices, and things to look for in classrooms, as well as identify educational practices to reconsider. (To best incorporate pedagogical practices, reading comprehension and content knowledge are presented in one book.) These books were developed to support professional growth, enhance engagement, and provide support in designing instruction that incorporates the best researched-based strategies.

This research base and understanding are integral to instruction in today's classrooms. Yet, despite a general knowledge of these ideas, many students continue to be plagued by inadequate literacy skills. Pulling from the work of educators, psychologists, neurologists, special educators, and more, our hope is that a renewed focus on the science ("body of facts or truths") of literacy will support a change in instructional practices and lead to higher literacy achievement.

> " Being an expert reader doesn't make you an expert about reading. That is why there is a science of reading: to understand this complex skill at levels that intuition cannot easily penetrate "
> —Mark Seidenberg (2017, 4)

Seminal Works to Build Understanding

Foundational works set the tone for understanding how research illuminates the pathway for instruction within the classroom. These seminal, theoretical pieces of research are widely recognized and serve as the guides to the books in this series. We will begin the journey with research and theories from the mid-1980s. Philip Gough and William Tunmer's seminal model of how young people learn to read, the Simple View of Reading (SVR), builds our understanding in a simple and usable manner. This widely used model has been manipulated to support new models since its origination. The Simple View of Reading articulates the basic components of how people become comprehenders of text.

Figure I.2—Simple View of Reading

Research indicating that reading comprehension is the product of decoding (word-level reading) and language comprehension is showcased in an equation that defines the skills needed to become a reader (Gough and Tunmer 1986). The idea presented by the SVR is that strong reading comprehension depends on the strong presence of both decoding and language comprehension skills. When one or the other is absent, reading comprehension will not occur. Although they are depicted simply in figure I.2, the skill domains of decoding and language comprehension include complex constructs that need to be understood separately and in relation to other constructs. *Decoding* (word-level reading) includes print concepts, phonological awareness, phonics and word recognition, and word knowledge. *Language comprehension* includes background knowledge, academic language, academic vocabulary, inferential language skills, and narrative language skills. Intentionally represented as multiplicative rather than additive, the Simple View of Reading highlights that reading comprehension is a result of both successful decoding and comprehension.

In 2001, Hollis Scarborough expanded on the foundation of the SVR to better support parents in understanding how children acquire the skills to be successful readers. Her Reading Rope shows how the skills of word recognition and language comprehension come together to support proficient reading. Not only are the many components of decoding and language comprehension interrelated, the two skill areas must be integrated for reading comprehension to take place.

The lower strands of the rope represent *word recognition*, weaving together phonological awareness (awareness of sounds within words), decoding (an understanding that sounds are encoded and decoded by the alphabet), and sight recognition (automaticity with frequently used words). These strands braid together as the portion of the rope that ties print to text.

The upper strands of the rope signify *language comprehension*. These include background and content knowledge, vocabulary, language structures, verbal reasoning, and literacy knowledge. These strands articulate the range of comprehension skills, strategies, and knowledge that support reading with fluency and understanding.

These intertwined strands symbolize the skills of fluent reading.

Figure I.3—Scarborough's Reading Rope

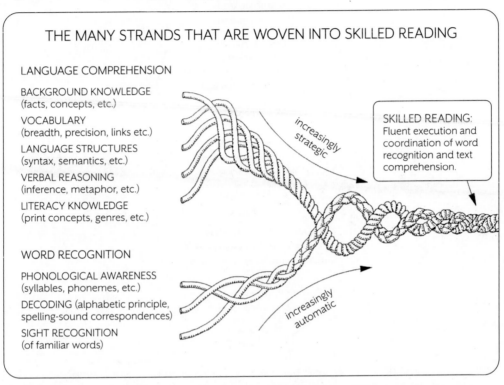

THE MANY STRANDS THAT ARE WOVEN INTO SKILLED READING

LANGUAGE COMPREHENSION

BACKGROUND KNOWLEDGE
(facts, concepts, etc.)

VOCABULARY
(breadth, precision, links etc.)

LANGUAGE STRUCTURES
(syntax, semantics, etc.)

VERBAL REASONING
(inference, metaphor, etc.)

LITERACY KNOWLEDGE
(print concepts, genres, etc.)

WORD RECOGNITION

PHONOLOGICAL AWARENESS
(syllables, phonemes, etc.)

DECODING (alphabetic principle,
spelling-sound correspondences)

SIGHT RECOGNITION
(of familiar words)

increasingly strategic

increasingly automatic

SKILLED READING:
Fluent execution and coordination of word recognition and text comprehension.

Credit: Hollis Scarborough, "Connecting Early Language and Literacy to Later Reading (Dis)abilities: Evidence, Theory, and Practice" in *Handbook of Research in Early Literacy*, edited by Susan B. Neuman and David K. Dickinson © Guilford Press, 2001. Used with permission.

Researchers have continued to develop and articulate models of how reading works. In 2021, Nell Duke and Kelly Cartwright introduced the Active View of Reading, a powerful model that extends the understandings from both the Simple View of Reading and Scarborough's Reading Rope. The Active View of Reading model recognizes the intersection between word recognition and language comprehension, referring to this intersection as the bridging processes. These processes are a departure from previous models, as they articulate the relationship and authentic merging of word recognition and language comprehension. The Active View of Reading also includes active self-regulation, which impacts word recognition, bridging processes, and language comprehension. Active self-regulation includes motivation and engagement, as well as executive function skills and the use of strategies.

Figure I.4—Duke and Cartwright's Active View of Reading

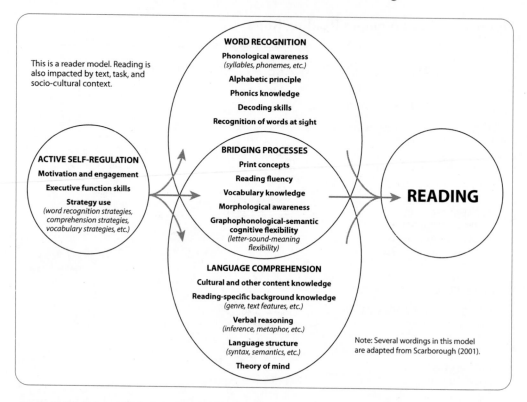

This is a reader model. Reading is also impacted by text, task, and socio-cultural context.

WORD RECOGNITION
Phonological awareness
(syllables, phonemes, etc.)
Alphabetic principle
Phonics knowledge
Decoding skills
Recognition of words at sight

ACTIVE SELF-REGULATION
Motivation and engagement
Executive function skills
Strategy use
(word recognition strategies,
comprehension strategies,
vocabulary strategies, etc.)

BRIDGING PROCESSES
Print concepts
Reading fluency
Vocabulary knowledge
Morphological awareness
Graphophonological-semantic
cognitive flexibility
(letter-sound-meaning
flexibility)

READING

LANGUAGE COMPREHENSION
Cultural and other content knowledge
Reading-specific background knowledge
(genre, text features, etc.)
Verbal reasoning
(inference, metaphor, etc.)
Language structure
(syntax, semantics, etc.)
Theory of mind

Note: Several wordings in this model are adapted from Scarborough (2001).

Credit: Nell K. Duke and Kelly B. Cartwright, "The Science of Reading Progresses: Communicating Advances Beyond the Simple View of Reading." *Reading Research Quarterly*, Vol. 56: Issue S1. © 2021 The Authors. Used with permission.

Each of these theoretical frameworks helps educators understand the essential components that need to be part of instruction as students learn to read. Moving beyond these frameworks, a nuanced understanding of how the brain navigates print to master the reading process supports effective instruction. Numerous researchers have written about the phases of predictable reading development (Ehri 1995; Ehri and McCormick 1998; Ehri and Snowling 2004). These phases, supported by instruction, provide readers with the ability to recognize words "by sight." The phases include the following:

- **Prealphabetic reading:** Reader uses a range of visual clues, such as a picture or a logo, to "read" words. Reader does not yet understand the letter-sound relationship.

- **Partial alphabetic reading and writing:** Reader uses some grapheme-phoneme, or letter-sound, connections. This is known as *phonetic cue reading*. At this stage, the connections are not fully reliable.

- **Full alphabetic reading and writing:** Reader has basic sound/symbol correspondences and attends to every letter in every word. At this stage, readers can convert letters into sounds and words.

- **Consolidated alphabetic reading:** Reader has some sight vocabulary and a breadth of strategies to read unknown words. Reader uses chunks of words to support the reading of words.

- **Automatic reading:** Reader is skilled and recognizes most words. Unfamiliar words are approached with a variety of strategies.

Orthographic Mapping

Another term for how words are retrieved is *orthographic mapping*. According to David Kilpatrick, "Orthographic mapping is the process readers use to store written words for immediate, effortless retrieval. It is the means by which readers turn unfamiliar words into familiar, instantaneously accessible sight words" (2015, 81). In orthographic mapping, readers use the oral language processing part of their brains to match phonemes (sounds within words) to the letters found inside words. As this mapping becomes more fluent, readers can instantly recognize words.

Five Essential Components

Research continues in the field of education. In 2000, the National Reading Panel (NRP) published its review of studies to identify the components of effective reading instruction. This comprehensive report carefully examined a wide range of research. Within its narrative about how readers develop, the NRP's report (2000a) articulated five essential components of reading:

- **Phonemic Awareness:** manipulating individual speech sounds
- **Phonics:** matching sounds to letters for use in reading and spelling
- **Fluency:** reading connected text accurately and fluently
- **Vocabulary:** knowing the meaning of words in speech and print
- **Reading Comprehension:** understanding what is read

Since the report was published, further research has only added to the body of research that supports the findings. The bottom line? Research continues to highlight the importance of integrated approaches to literacy instruction that include the five essential components in an intertwined way. Ultimately, the best ways to ensure students become engaged and successful readers and writers have not changed significantly.

This foundational information lays the groundwork for continued understanding of how to engage students with solid literacy instruction. Several institutions provide briefs or guides that present research in easily digestible formats. The Institute of Educational Sciences/What Works Clearinghouse Practice Guides provide educators with sound instructional practices related to a range of literacy skills. Additionally, the International Literacy Association provides Leadership Briefs that highlight integral pedagogy with a strong research base.

The Focus on Word Recognition

The English language has an alphabetic writing system that is filled with complexities and nuances, rules and exceptions. For students to understand what they read, they must be able to access the words on the page. This requires explicit instruction on how letters work and how words work. Students need consistent opportunities to engage with new phonemic awareness and decoding skills, as well as ample time to read and reread for fluency. The instruction must be presented systematically, in an order that allows for students to move into more complex skills as they master simpler skills.

Word recognition encompasses a range of skills that must weave together for successful reading. That is why word recognition is an integral part of the Simple View of Reading equation and the bottom strand of Scarborough's Reading Rope. Teachers can ensure reading success for their students by entrenching them in the important and fundamental components that lead to successful word recognition. These key components include phonological awareness, phonics (decoding), sight word recognition, and fluency.

According to the What Works Clearinghouse practice guide *Foundational Skills to Support Reading for Understanding in Kindergarten Through 3rd Grade* (Foorman et al. 2016), research finds strong evidence for the need to do the following:

- Develop awareness of the segments of sounds in speech and how they link to letters.
- Teach students to decode words, analyze word parts, and write and recognize words.

Further, the report indicates moderate evidence that reading connected text daily supports reading accuracy, fluency, and comprehension; additional evidence supports teaching academic language skills.

Word Recognition Progressions

Word recognition skills are most effectively attained in a systematic progression. Therefore, systematic instruction should align with the progressions shown in figures I.5 and I.6.

Figure I.5—Phonological Awareness Progression

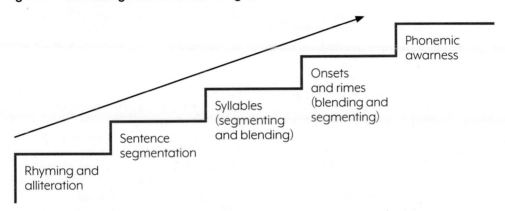

Figure I.6—Phonemic Awareness Progression

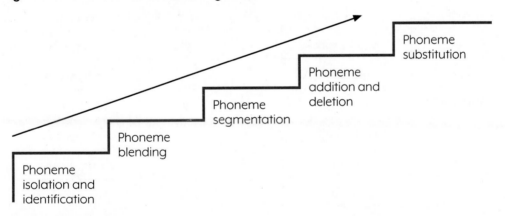

Recognized Phonemes

Phonemes are the individual, unique units of sound in the English language. These sounds help distinguish words and meanings of words. Letters and combinations of letters, or *graphemes*, represent each of these sounds. See figure I.7. **Note:** Due to accents and dialects, there are lists that vary from this specific representation.

Figure I.7—Recognized Phonemes

Symbol	Sound		Symbol	Sound
/ā/	angel, rain		/g/	gift, dog
/ă/	cat, apple		/h/	happy, hat
/ē/	eat, seed		/j/	jump, bridge
/ĕ/	echo, red		/l/	lip, fall
/ī/	island, light		/m/	mother, home
/ĭ/	in, sit		/n/	nose, on
/ō/	oatmeal, bone		/p/	pencil, pop
/ŏ/	octopus, mom		/r/	rain, care
/u/	up, hum		/s/	soup, face
/ōo/	oodles, moon		/t/	time, cat
/ŏo/	put, book		/v/	vine, of
/ə/	above, sofa		/wh/	what, why
/oi/, /oy/	oil, boy		/w/	wet, wind
/ou/, /ow/	out, cow		/y/	yes, beyond
/aw/, /ô/	awful, caught		/z/	zoo, because
/är/	car, far		/th/	thing, health
/ôr/	four, or		/th/	this, brother
/ûr/	her, bird, turn		/sh/	shout, machine
/b/	baby, crib		/zh/	pleasure, vision
/k/	cup, stick		/ch/	children, scratch
/d/	dog, end		/ng/	ring, finger
/f/	phone, golf			

Credit: Hallie Kay Yopp and Ruth Helen Yopp, *Purposeful Play for Early Childhood Phonological Awareness*, 2nd ed. © Shell Education, 2022. Used with permission.

Settled Science

When considering the body of research that is now known as the Science of Reading, there are implications for instruction that can be considered settled. David Kilpatrick notes, "We teach reading in different ways; [students] learn to read proficiently in only one way" (2015, 39). Recognizing that certain pedagogies and practices are settled science allows all educators to infuse them in their instruction. Instruction must be:

Evidence-based: Instruction and materials are anchored in trustworthy and reliable evidence. The evidence should indicate a consistent success record in increasing students' literacy abilities. Practices should build skills in phonemic awareness, phonics, vocabulary development, reading fluency (including oral skills), and reading comprehension.

Explicit: Instruction should include direct teaching that provides explanations of the concepts, modeling of the concepts, and practice with the concepts. Instruction should be clear, specific, and directly connected to an objective.

Systematic: Instruction should follow thoughtfully planned instructional routines. These routines should be planned in advance, ensuring maximum time on task.

Sequential: Instruction should teach skills and concepts sequentially from easiest to hardest. Foundational skills are taught to support higher-order skills. Sequencing should be intentional within and across grades.

> " It is called *explicit* because it is an unambiguous and direct approach to teaching that includes both instructional design and delivery procedures.
> —Anita Archer (2011, 1) "

Rigorous for all: Instruction must include complex texts and tasks for all students. Referring to the practice of having students only read books at "their level," Sue Pimentel (2018) notes, "The texts they're reading don't require them to decipher unfamiliar vocabulary, confront challenging concepts, or parse new and complicated language" (2018, para. 5). Every student needs opportunities to engage with difficult vocabulary to build their knowledge, and difficult tasks to heighten their skills.

Intentional: Instruction should thoughtfully align to grade-level standards, and it should be scaffolded to support student needs. Assessment provides an understanding of what students know and what they need to know.

Engaging: Instruction should ensure students have clear understanding of the objectives. It should enable students to make connections to their out-of-school lives and see the relevance of the work. Instruction should provide students with challenges and opportunities to take risks (Jackson and Zmuda 2014).

Designed to build knowledge: Instruction should be designed to build knowledge, vocabulary, and understanding about a range of topics. In a brief for the Knowledge Matters Campaign, Daniel Willingham notes, "Students need deep knowledge of a subject in order to think creatively or critically about it" (2016, 1).

Aligned to the essential components: Instruction must be aligned to the integral components of literacy instruction as indicated by the evidence. It should focus on the five essential components showcased by the NRP. Written expression (composition) and oral language (speaking and listening) are also essential components of literacy.

From the Classroom

What is the power of a letter? Moreover, what is the power of learning a letter and its sound? Let me tell you, for a first grader, the answer is *immense*. Several years ago, while Jen was serving as the Director of Literacy, she was visiting classrooms, supporting teachers and students using a systematic and explicit phonics program combined with decodable readers. She visited a busy classroom, filled with active first graders. As she entered the room, she was greeted with smiles and the buzz of learning.

Within a few moments, Jen knew what was happening. The letter *i* was plastered around the classroom, in multiple places. A word list that included *win*, *Kip*, *pig*, *big*, and *wig* was prominently displayed on the front wall. Students were reading—with enthusiasm, with energy. There was an air of unbridled excitement in the room. Students practiced the letter name and its sound, found it in words, and used it in short sentences. Students had mini whiteboards in their laps and were writing short vowel *i* words, then drawing "quick pics" of a range of words prompted by the teacher.

The letter *i* opened doors to reading and gave joy to learning. That systematic and explicit process was providing students with a natural pathway to discover more words, uncover more language, and learn. Soon after the explicit lesson was over, students engaged in a range of activities to reinforce their learning. Jen worked her way around the room, pausing when a six-year-old exclaimed, "Hey Mrs. Lady, watch me read this book!" She kneeled down and listened to a new reader reading. Proud. Loud. "Kip hit it. What will Kip pick?" The words rang clearly and Jen smiled along with this newly confident reader. This integral step in becoming a reader had been learned, practiced, and was on its way to mastery.

Navigating This Book

Each of the first five chapters of this book showcases important research that supports the instruction of word recognition in the classroom. This includes literacy, mathematics, science, and social studies classrooms.

Chapter 1	Phonological Awareness
Chapter 2	Phonics—Systematic and Explicit
Chapter 3	Beyond Foundational Phonics—Multisyllabic Words and More
Chapter 4	Sight Recognition—Familiar Words
Chapter 5	Fluency

These chapters are structured to bridge the gap between the science of literacy instruction and classroom practice. Each chapter begins by examining the research with a thoughtful and critical eye. Following the research, you will find instructional implications. These implications identify how the research should impact the work of educators in classrooms today. Next, you will find key terms for teacher understanding. Each of these key terms is defined and showcased in a classroom example.

Each chapter also includes research-based instructional strategies. These strategies are aligned to grade-level bands. However, many of these strategies have utility across grade levels and can be modified to support students beyond the bands suggested. Each chapter closes with the following sections:

- **Top Must-Dos:** A summary of research implications, the must-do list supports all teachers as they navigate taking the science of reading directly into their classrooms.

- **Further Considerations:** Offering additional insights about effective instruction, this section also includes (as appropriate) guidance for moving away from practices that are not supported by research.

- **Reflection Questions:** A short list of questions to use as conversation starters for professional learning or for self-reflection.

The final chapter in this book, written by guest author Alan Becker, explores how to seize every opportunity to take word recognition instruction beyond the language arts block and discover the power of cross-content connections.

Take a deep breath. While we as educators do not have a Hippocratic oath, we know the great responsibility we face each day. Louisa Moats (2020b) said it best: "Teaching reading is rocket science." Let's build the literacy rocket together.

Phonological Awareness

From the Classroom

I created a matching activity for my students as they worked in a small group to reinforce their phonological awareness of beginning sounds. This small group had been engaged in explicit learning of initial sound matching. Students had seen the process modeled, had practiced it with me, and were now ready to practice independently. I created several pairs of cards with pictures on them. Each matching pair had an object on it that began with the same initial sound. Some of the pictures were:

a bear and a ball

a hammer and a hand

a ring and a robot

a sun and a spoon

a frog and a fan

Each student in the group was handed one card with a picture on it. They were given a moment to identify the picture and say the word inside their head. I supported students with any vocabulary they needed to find success. Then, each student was directed to find the person who had a picture card with the same initial sound as theirs. I watched as they found their partner with the matching initial sound. When all students found their matches, each pair showed their pictures, said their words, and identified the initial sound. The small group repeated the findings for additional practice.

—Dani Battle
Former Second Grade Teacher
Walter P. Carter Elementary
Baltimore, Maryland

Background Information and Research

Stop for a minute, close your eyes, and listen. What do you hear? Most likely, you are surrounded by a variety of sounds that you can immediately recognize and name. From the moment we are born, we begin to experience our world through our senses, one of those being our ability to hear the sounds around us. As babies, we respond to our caregivers' voices by turning our heads. We may cry when hearing a loud or sharp noise for the first time. As we get older, we start to distinguish the natural sounds in our environment—a car horn, a dog's bark, the boom of thunder before a storm—and we also begin to imitate patterns of sounds that have been repeated to us in spoken language. "Ba ba," "wa wa," "ma ma," and "da da" are a cause for celebration as baby's first words. More importantly, these babblings are the first steps in a child's recognition that speech consists of sounds. This knowledge of, attention to, and manipulation of the sounds of language is the precursor to word recognition and is known as *phonological awareness*. Phonological awareness begins to develop before formal schooling, and continues through the primary grades. It is a foundation for students to be successful readers (Kilpatrick, 2016).

Although this recognition, response, and repetition of sound happens naturally for most children as they grow older, learning to connect what is heard and spoken to the print seen on a page is a learned process that must be taught and developed in a systematic, explicit way.

Connection to the Rope

As we considered in the Introduction, Scarborough's Reading Rope (2001) provides a visual representation of the way word recognition and language comprehension intertwine like a rope, showing how these skills combine to create automatic and strategic readers. These two components must be integrated in reading instruction to develop reading comprehension. *Phonological awareness* is one of the parts of the printed word recognition strand of the Reading Rope. Automaticity in word recognition skills, beginning with phonological awareness, is required for students to become skilled, fluent readers.

Implications for Teaching and Learning

Teachers need an in-depth understanding of the meaning of *phonological awareness* and its components as they prepare for its use in reading instruction in their classrooms. There is sometimes confusion between phonological awareness and phonics (defined in Chapter 2). *Phonological awareness* is the ability to attend to and manipulate the sounds of spoken language (Yopp and Yopp 2022). An important distinction from *phonics* is that phonological awareness focuses ONLY on *hearing* speech sounds, with little to no print or meaning included. Another key distinction in the definition is the "ability to manipulate sounds." This means that students must be able to perform cognitive tasks using the units of sound. For example, if a teacher tells a student to replace the beginning sound in *cat* with a /b/ sound, the student should say the word *bat*. To enhance a student's phonological awareness, this activity would be done orally, with no print involved.

There are multiple skills required for *phonological* awareness, as illustrated in the umbrella diagram shown in figure 1.1. The discrete skills shown on the left side, presented in order from simple to complex, include distinguishing words in sentences, having syllable awareness, recognizing rhyming and alliteration, and segregating onset and rime. On the right side of the umbrella are the components of *phonemic* awareness, a type of phonological awareness (see Key Terms for Teacher Understanding on page 24). They include the tasks of segmenting, blending, isolating, and manipulating phonemes.

Figure 1.1—Umbrella Structure of Phonological Awareness

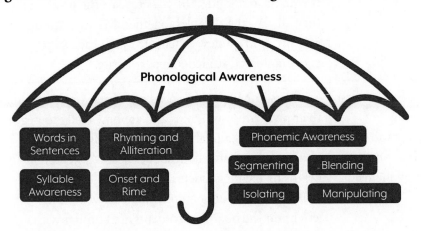

Research shows that phonological awareness is essential for the development of reading because of the relationship between the spoken word and the written word, and that phonological awareness of the sounds of spoken language is required to learn letter-sound correspondence (Ehri et al. 2001; Kilpatrick 2015, 2016; Moats 2020a; Yopp and Yopp 2022). Due to the importance of phonological awareness in literacy development and reading achievement, instruction in phonological awareness must be systematic and explicit, with opportunities built in for teachers to assess, reteach, and continuously scaffold and review.

Key Terms for Teacher Understanding

The following chart provides definitions of essential terms educators need to know and an example of each one.

Term and Definition	Example
explicit instruction—skills are taught directly to students through lessons with clear objectives and guided practice with scaffolded support	Ms. Strawbridge's phonological awareness focus lesson today is on syllable segmentation. Ms. Strawbridge explains that words are made up of parts you can hear, called *syllables*. Each syllable will have a vowel sound. You can clap to it, like a beat. To explicitly practice this skill, Ms. Strawbridge models first by saying her last name, "Strawbridge," out loud and then asks students to repeat her name. She says her name a second time, this time clapping with each syllable—*Straw/bridge* (two claps). Students repeat her name and clap the syllables—*Straw/bridge* (two claps). Then each student takes turns saying their first name out loud. The class repeats the name, and they all clap the syllables together. Ms. Strawbridge supports and guides students through each step, encouraging all students to participate.
grapheme—the smallest unit in a writing system; a letter and/or letter combination that represents a phoneme	Students in Ms. Jensen's class have been working on their phonemic awareness and are now ready to begin including their alphabet letter knowledge through phoneme-grapheme correspondence. Ms. Jensen begins by having students match initial phonemes to the corresponding graphemes. She writes the letter *j* on the board, as students are familiar with the beginning letter of her last name: /j/ *Jensen*. She then orally lists words that begin with that phoneme/grapheme, such as students' names and objects in the room (*Jason, Jill, juice, jeans, jump,* and so on). This helps scaffold learning from the concrete to the abstract and allows her to differentiate and increase the difficulty of words as they proceed.

Term and Definition	Example
isolation, deletion, and manipulation—phoneme *isolation* is the ability to isolate or separate sounds at different positions within a word, such as initial, medial, and final; phoneme *manipulation* is the ability to add, delete, or substitute phonemes in spoken words	Isolation Activity: During a game of "I Spy," Umi was using her ability to isolate sounds to locate an item in the classroom that began with the /t/ sound. Umi located a table, a top, and a tub. She shared the items she found with her tablemates. As the activity continued, Umi played "I Spy" to practice isolating medial and then ending sounds: • middle, or medial, sounds: /ŏ/ = *dog, block, sock, clock* • ending, or final, sounds: /d/ = *red, seed, bird, end* Manipulation Activity: It is important to write out the phoneme manipulations beforehand as it is usually too difficult to try and think of words and sounds on the spot. Umi's teacher made up a song, in which she sings, "Add ___ to ___ to make ___." Students practice by singing, "Add /t/ to *in* to make *tin*." For deleting an initial sound from a word, the teacher sings, "Say ___. Take away the ___ sound and now ___ is ___." Students practice by singing, "Say *cat*. Take away the /k/ sound, and now *cat* is *at*." To practice substituting an initial sound, she sings, "Change the ___ in ___ to ___. Your new word is___." Students practice, "Change the /r/ in *red* to /b/. Your new word is *bed*."

(Continued)

Term and Definition	Example
onset—the part of a syllable that comes before the vowel; an onset can be a consonant or a blend; some syllables do not have an onset **rime**—the part of a syllable that includes the vowel and any consonants that follow; all syllables have a rime because all syllables have a vowel sound	Mrs. Dawson begins onset-rime instruction with one-syllable words. She has students sit or stand in a circle on the carpet so she can incorporate movement and quickly assess each student as they blend the onset and rime to create the correct word. She orally divides a word into its onset and rime. As she says the onset, she pats her right leg (providing a mirror image for her students). As she says the rime, she pats her left leg. Then as she blends the onset and rime together, she slides her hands down her legs to her feet and says the word all together. She models this with a few words before calling on students to try words on their own or lead the group in onset-rime practice with her help. Examples of onset-rimes: • b-and • c-up

Term and Definition	Example
orthographic mapping—the process used to store words in long-term memory; a cognitive task where readers make connections between phonemes (sounds) and graphemes (letters) to combine and recall the pronunciation, meaning, and spelling of words quickly and effortlessly	Miss Greene uses manipulatives such as popper fidgets (fidgets made from silicone dimples that push in and out). First, she says a word out loud. Students repeat the word. Miss Greene models counting the phonemes and asks students to count them with her. Students pop bubbles as they say the sounds they hear, to correspond with each phoneme in the word. Miss Greene next writes the word on the board, mapping the phonemes to the graphemes. She says the word aloud again and has students say the phonemes as she underlines the graphemes that correspond. Miss Greene then distributes activity sheets with sound boxes (also known as Elkonin boxes), along with chips. Students place the chips in the boxes to map the sounds. At first, the number of boxes corresponds to the number of phonemes. As skill levels increase, Miss Greene uses activity sheets with more boxes than phonemes.

(Continued)

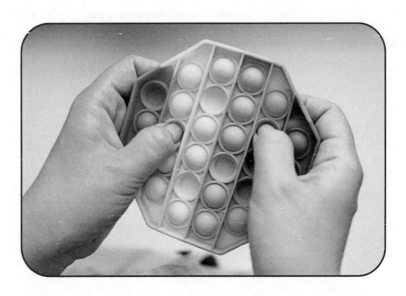

Term and Definition	Example
phoneme/phonemic awareness—the awareness of the smallest units of sound (phonemes) and the ability to manipulate those sounds	Ms. Penland knows it is important to complete phoneme awareness activities orally, and that she must make sure her students understand phonemes are sounds, not to be confused with written letters. For this reason, she likes to incorporate pictures in her beginning phoneme awareness lessons. Ms. Penland has laminated multiple picture cards for identifying positions of phonemes in words, beginning with the initial phoneme. She models by posting pictures of a duck and a car. She says the phoneme /k/ and points to the picture of the car, then says the phoneme /d/ and points to the picture of the duck. She distributes cards with pictures of a dog, a cat, a bear, and a fish, and each student lays them out on their desk. As Ms. Penland says a phoneme, students hold up the picture that begins with that sound. For example, Ms. Penland says the phoneme /k/, and students hold up the picture of the cat. They repeat the activity with the /f/ phoneme. Ms. Penland uses the activity in small groups and has students practice in pairs. Later, she can increase the rigor by addressing phonemes in different positions.

Term and Definition	Example
phoneme—the smallest unit of sound in spoken word, usually characterized by these marks / /; there are 44 phonemes in the English language	Mr. Ngo is reviewing the number of phonemes in a word. He begins using words with one phoneme. He models first with the word *I*. As he says the word out loud, he holds up one finger to represent one phoneme, /ī/. He repeats this process with the word *a* = /ā/. He continues this process, gradually increasing the number of phonemes in the words. For each increase, he models first. He watches the class carefully, and if he feels a word will be difficult, he asks the whole class to show the number of fingers at once to represent the phonemes. If they have done the word before or if the word has more easily identifiable phonemes, he will ask for volunteers or call on a student. Phoneme examples: • it = /ĭ/ /t/ = 2 • ate = /ā/ /t/ = 2 • big = /b/ /ĭ/ /g/ = 3 • stop = /s/ /t/ /ŏ/ /p/ = 4

(Continued)

Term and Definition	Example
phonological awareness—the awareness of (attention to and manipulation of) the sounds of spoken language	Ms. Rowland teaches lessons to develop phonological awareness in her kindergarten classroom each day. She follows either the scope and sequence (see definition on page 31) provided by her school district or a research-based phonological awareness continuum. Phonological awareness relates only to the sounds of language and not to print.
	First, Ms. Rowland teaches her students word awareness. She finds a familiar chant that they know, such as *Five Little Ducks*. She says the chant correctly first, and students repeat it after her. She then tells them every time they hear the word *duck(s)*, they should cover their mouths with their hands: *Five little…went out one day*. After they chant with the deletion of a word, they substitute or replace the word *ducks* with *chicks*: *Five little chicks went out one day*. This helps students work on understanding that sentences are made up of words and is a precursor to deleting and substituting letter sounds later.
rhyme—the correspondence of sound between words or the ending of words	Isabella likes when her teacher uses nursery rhymes, songs, and poems to work on rhyme, rhythm, and repetition. This week is one of Isabella's favorites, "Twinkle, Twinkle, Little Star" by Jane Taylor. Isabella listens to Mrs. Jung read through each stanza of the poem once. Mrs. Jung explains that as she reads the lines, she will stop and ask students which rhyming words they heard. In the first two lines, Isabella is quick to raise her hand because she hears the rhyming words, *star* and *are*. Isabella also hears *high* and *sky*, *gone* and *upon*, *light* and *night*, *dark* and *spark*, and *go* and *so*.

Term and Definition	Example
scope and sequence—an organized curriculum designed with systematic and explicit instruction that includes repetition and review	At the start of the school year, each teacher receives a scope and sequence to help guide the progression of the daily reading lessons. The scope and sequence is structured to include daily direct instruction, beginning with simple reading skills and moving to more complex skills as students develop mastery. Repetition and review are included as needed. Sometimes, a scope and sequence is called a *curriculum map*. This is an example of a six-week scope and sequence for phonological awareness: • Week 1 Focus: Sound Discrimination • Week 2 Focus: Word Discrimination • Week 3 Focus: Rhyming and Alliteration • Week 4 Focus: Sentence Segmentation • Week 5 Focus: Syllable Segmentation • Week 6 Focus: Onset and Rime
systematic instruction—intentionally sequenced lessons and activities to ensure skill mastery	Mr. Griffin has been systematically teaching blending and segmentation in phonological awareness. He is ready to design lessons for learning the positions of sounds in words. He knows that the easiest sound to recognize is the beginning, or initial, sound, such as /d/ in *dog*, so he focuses on that skill first. The next easiest skill is the ending, or final, sound of the word, such as /g/ in *dog*, so he plans activities for final sounds for two days later. The most difficult position for sounds in words is the medial, or middle, sound, such as /ŏ/ in *dog*. He plans activities for medial sounds for the following week. Mr. Griffin knows that he must scaffold these skills from the simple to the complex and build in time for review or reteaching if needed.

Hop! Sentence Segmenting

Grades: K–1

Description

Students physically hop each time they hear a new word in a sentence: one hop equals one word.

Rationale

This strategy reinforces the concept that sentences are made of words, engaging students in a physical representation of segmenting sentences into words. By having students' movements correspond with each word in a sentence, they become more aware of the stopping and starting of words, the number of syllables words have, and the spaces between words in sentences.

Process

1. Decide on the context for using this strategy, and plan ahead. Consider the following questions:

   - Is there enough room in the classroom, or do you need to go to a larger room or outside? You will need space for students to hop. They will also be excited to move around and jump, so it could get noisy.

   - Are you going to place students in small groups to complete the activity? If students are in small groups, they could spread out a little more, making it easier for you to observe them as they hop.

   - Students will be assigned to small groups. While one group is hopping, what will the other groups be doing? The other students can be counting the words, holding up their fingers or clapping, knowing they will be asked to share the number of words in the sentence when the group is done. They need to be actively involved in some way as they observe the group that is participating.

2. Prepare at least two or more short sentences for each group that hops, depending on how much time you have for this lesson. Begin with sentences that have only one-syllable words, such as: *The dog barks.* Then add rounds that incorporate multisyllabic words, such as: *I enjoy swimming at the pool.*

3. Model how students will hop to show the words in the sentence. Tell them you are pretending to be a bunny, and as you say a sentence, hop forward one time as you say each word.

4. Have students in the first group line up to begin the activity. Tell the second group they will be counting or clapping as the other group hops. Model the process by choosing one student from each group to demonstrate hopping and clapping or counting.

5. Ask all students to listen as you say the sentence first. Remind them to count the words silently in their minds as they listen to help them get ready. Have students repeat the sentence.

6. Say the sentence again. This time, as students repeat the sentence, tell them to hop forward as they say each word (one hop = one word). Have students try to say the words and hop in unison.

7. Monitor as students hop to assess whether any students are struggling and in need of extra support.

8. After they have completed the sentence, ask students to tell you in unison on the count of three (including the ones who were observing) how many times they hopped, or how many words they counted in the sentence. You can also have them hold up the number of fingers that corresponds to the number of words instead of saying it verbally.

9. Repeat a new sentence with each group.

10. Debrief the activity with students by asking them to share what they want to remember about words and sentences.

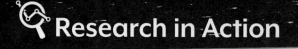

Differentiation

- If students need more structured space to hop, hallway squares, carpet squares, or taped boundaries could be used to delineate the area where they should hop each time.

- If space is an issue, have each student use a paper bunny and a number line at their desk. Students can hop the bunnies forward on the line as they say the sentence.

- Increase the complexity of this strategy by using sentences with more words or by adding multisyllabic words.

- Have students take turns leading the activity, using their own sentences.

- This activity can also be used in a variety of additional ways, such as with sounds, phonemes, or rhyming phrases.

Word Squish

Grades: 2–3

Description

Students listen to hear segmented phonemes and isolated sounds in words, and then place balls of play dough in Elkonin boxes (sound boxes) for each phoneme and squish the dough. The number of Elkonin boxes aligns with the number of phonemes. For example, for the word *crab*, there are four phonemes (/k/ /r/ /ă/ /b/), so there should be four boxes.

An example of an Elkonin box is shown below (figure 1.2). A picture of the word can be placed above the box if desired. For phoneme awareness, students only need to hear the word, not write it.

Figure 1.2—Sample Elkonin Boxes

Rationale

Word Squish provides a hands-on, tactile way for students to segment words into phonemes. Pushing on the play dough takes more effort and intentional movement than simply placing counters or other manipulatives in Elkonin boxes. Students must move the play dough to the correct space and squish it as they practice word segmentation and phoneme isolation. This purposeful repetition of movement in conjunction with a novel and playful activity increases the likelihood of storage in long-term memory.

Process

1. Preplan according to the context of teaching this strategy and the materials that will be used. Consider the following questions:

   - Will you teach this strategy to the whole class or in small groups? What will the other students be doing while you work with a small group? Small groups will allow for closer monitoring and support for struggling students.

   - What will your Elkonin boxes look like? They could be pre-made and laminated or drawn on large-size graph paper. They could have the exact number of boxes corresponding to the phonemes in the words you choose, or they could have more boxes than phonemes.

   - How much play dough do you need? How will you store it? Be clear about the expectations for using the play dough, and model how students should use it. Have them practice before beginning the activity.

2. Distribute the materials. This may not be the first time students have experienced Elkonin boxes, but it may be the first time in school they use play dough. Allow time for students to manipulate and play with the dough before starting the lesson. Have students put all the play dough on the paper before you begin.

3. Model how to squish the play dough into the Elkonin boxes as you segment the phonemes in each word. Show how to place a small ball of play dough in the outlined square of the Elkonin box on the paper and squish the ball. Have students practice on their own or with partners. The class may need to first practice segmenting the phonemes a different way. For example, students could practice by using tokens or chips, or by clapping. Remind students that using play dough this way is another way to identify the phonemes.

4. When each student has finished their Word Squish, ask them how many phonemes they squished. Extend the activity by asking them to isolate a phoneme (beginning, medial, or ending) or by adding or substituting a phoneme.

5. Repeat this process with more words. Begin with segmentation, and then move to isolation.

6. Debrief this strategy by asking students to explain the connection between the squishing of the play dough and the sounds they heard in words. Ask them how they can adapt this strategy if they do not have any play dough with them.

Differentiation

- This strategy can be differentiated through its difficulty of skill level. Start with segmenting words with a small number of phonemes for students who struggle with phonemic awareness. Move to words with more phonemes, blends, digraphs, and long vowel patterns to increase the difficulty.

- When working with isolating phonemes, the initial sound is the easiest place to start. Next, work with the final sound, and then the middle or medial sound.

- When students are manipulating phonemes, provide different colors of dough to help students see the placement of the manipulated phonemes.

- For students who have sensory processing issues, manipulating counters into Elkonin boxes on a computer screen through an application such as Google Docs™ or Jamboard™ will allow for a similar hands-on experience.

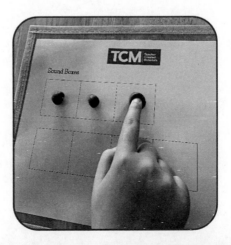

Sound Walls

Grades: K–3

Description

A Sound Wall displays sound cards with letters next to mouth articulation photos, pictures of students, and word cards or picture cards. It promotes connections between speech and print and fosters students' abilities to connect phonemes and graphemes. Sound walls are organized to showcase all phonemes. (Most research indicates there are 44.) With students, build a Sound Wall with a section for consonants and a "vowel valley," where the various vowel sounds are displayed. Examples of Sound Walls can be found online.

Rationale

A Sound Wall is used to support the connections between phonemes and orthographic patterns, and as a bridge between phonological awareness and phonics. It is designed to support students in the articulation of speech sounds (Bottari 2020) and helps anchor letter-sound knowledge.

Process

1. Choose a location in the classroom that will be visible to all students and that can be easily referenced.

2. Build the Sound Wall as phonemes are taught. Add the graphemes as they are introduced.

   • Begin with the common consonants and short vowels. As the letter is introduced, place a letter card along with a sound card on the wall.

   • Add mouth pictures next to the sound cards, further cluing students in to what their mouths are doing to produce a sound.

   • Add pictures of words that use that sound. Include examples that have the sound at the beginning, middle, and end of the word.

3. Have students use the Sound Wall to practice the sounds. Remember that repetition and play with the sounds will boost students' connections to the sounds.

4. Model for students how to use the Sound Wall to discover various ways to create the sound. Students can hear the sound, mimic how the mouth is shaped, and locate spelling patterns.

Differentiation

- Place a mirror (or mirrors) next to the sound wall. Have students use the mirror to watch themselves form the sounds, and use the sound wall as a guide.

- Say a sound and have students find it on the sound wall. Have partners work together to identify sounds.

- Create mini sound walls on large pieces of construction paper for students to have at their desks and take home for additional support.

Instruction for Higher Grade Levels

Phonological awareness instruction for intermediate and above-level students will likely be intervention to support gaps in understanding. (See page 41, "Provide Instruction beyond Second Grade as Needed.")

Moving Forward: Top Must-Dos

Phonological awareness lessons and activities should be carefully planned, purposeful, and engaging. They should be implemented in daily whole-group lessons, following a research-based scope and sequence. Lessons can also be delivered in small groups or individually to meet student needs.

Teach Phonological Awareness Sequentially and Explicitly

The Reading Rope (Scarborough 2001) shows teachers *what* to teach to support the development of skilled readers in their classrooms. The next step is to understand *how* to teach to support literacy development. Researchers agree there is substantial evidence showing a clear benefit from systematically, sequentially, and explicitly teaching children phonological awareness (Ehri et al. 2001; Kilpatrick 2015, 2016; Moats 2020a; Yopp and Yopp 2022). Designing a scope and sequence that focuses on the phonological awareness skills that build from easiest to hardest allows for students to connect what they already know to their new learning with each lesson. With direct, explicit instruction of the phonological awareness skills, teachers support their students through modeling, guided practice, immediate feedback, and reteaching if needed. Teacher language is specific and directly connected to the learning objective. Assessment and time for review of skills are also built into systematic instruction.

> The foundational word recognition skill of phonological awareness must be assessed regularly and should be done both formally and informally.

Assess Phonological Awareness Skills Regularly

If a strand in a physical rope becomes frayed or broken, the entire rope can become unraveled, and it may lose its strength. Likewise, if a strand in the Reading Rope (Scarborough 2001) is weak, then there could be a breakdown in overall reading comprehension. Therefore, the foundational word-recognition skill of phonological awareness must be assessed regularly and should be done both formally and informally. Assessing a student's progress through daily observation and interactions will provide teachers with regular information on mastery of skills, allow them to give timely feedback, reteach or review a concept or skill as needed, and decide which students are ready to move on to new learning. With regular progress monitoring, teachers are also able to differentiate within whole-group lessons as well as pull students into small groups for more scaffolded instruction. Documentation of assessment is the key to success for conversations with guardians or administrators when support is needed for struggling students. Keep this documentation in an anecdotal notebook or structured as a checklist of skills from the standards or scope and sequence, noted as mastered or not. See below for an example of an assessment checklist.

Student can isolate:	Yes	No
initial sounds		
medial sounds		
final sounds		
Student can:	**Yes**	**No**
substitute sounds		
delete sounds		
add sounds		

Provide Instruction beyond Second Grade as Needed

Although many curricular scope and sequences do not include phonological awareness in higher grades, students who struggle with the foundational literacy skill of word recognition may still need explicit instruction in this area. Research has identified specific skills within phonological awareness that teachers should focus on when targeting reading gaps in word recognition skills with older students (Moats 2020a; Reutzel 2015). Louisa Moats states, "Of all the phonological skills, the ability to identify, manipulate, and remember strings of speech sounds accounts for a significant portion of the difference between good readers and poor readers" (2020a, 57). When identifying which phonological and phonemic awareness skills to focus on with older students, consider these three areas: phoneme identification and isolation, blending and segmenting phonemes, and manipulating phonemes.

Further Considerations

Acknowledge the Two Sounds in Blends

Teachers sometimes confuse students by teaching blends as a unit of sound, but it is easier to teach students from the beginning that in a blend, we can distinctly hear the two sounds on their own. For example, in the word *tree*, *tr* is pronounced and heard separately as /t/ and /r/. This systematic, explicit instruction will also help students later distinguish two adjacent consonants that blend to form consonant digraphs from adjacent consonants that form one sound, such as the *ch* in *chip* = /ch/. When students begin to segment phonemes and practice phoneme-grapheme matching, knowing that a blend has two separate sounds could make this less difficult for some.

Phoneme Awareness Can Be Taught Prior to Introducing Graphemes

Phoneme awareness and phonics are not the same, although there is a synergy noted between the two (Duke and Mesmer 2018). Phoneme awareness is based on working with the units of sounds (phonemes) in language, and phonics focuses on the printed word—the letter or letters (graphemes) that correspond to each sound. Combining phoneme-level instruction with alphabet knowledge using orthographic mapping or Elkonin boxes, for example, is both effective and efficient in helping students understand the associations between phonemes and graphemes but is not necessary from day one. Many times, these skills and combination of strategies are not taught until after segmenting, blending, isolating, and manipulating phonemes are mastered. Once a strong grasp of phoneme awareness is noted, then corresponding graphemes should be introduced.

My Teaching Checklist

Are you ready to develop students' phonological awareness skills so they may be successful readers? Use this checklist to help you get started!

Phonological Awareness	
Look Fors	**Description**
Systematic and explicit instruction is provided.	• Develop a scope and sequence with logically sequenced skills, progressing from simple to complex. • Include direct teaching opportunities with clear objectives and modeling. • Infuse phonological awareness practice throughout the day.
Regular assessment that influences data-driven instruction is being implemented.	• Intentionally monitor progress and check in with students while they work each day. • Document formal and informal observations of student progress. • Give immediate feedback to students when needed. • Build time into the scope and sequence for review and reteaching. • Provide small-group instruction when needed. • Differentiate activities for students when applicable.

Chapter Summary

Phonological awareness is a key component to the teaching of reading. It represents a foundational literacy skill for students to increase their automaticity in word recognition as they become more proficient readers. Researchers agree that students with poor phonological awareness usually struggle with reading, especially as they get older (Ehri et al. 2001; Kilpatrick 2015, 2016; Moats 2020a; Seidenberg 2017; Willingham 2017; Yopp and Yopp 2022). Phonological awareness skills focus on the understanding of, attention to, and manipulation of the sounds of language and must be taught in an explicit, systematic way. For many students, the time spent learning phonological awareness will be their first exposure in a school environment to being taught to read. The implication of this knowledge is important for teachers to remember as they plan their instruction. Focusing on the spoken word provides opportunities for teachers to be playful with language and plan engaging lessons incorporating alliteration, rhyme, and rhythm with songs, poems, and familiar nursery rhymes that students may have heard before and enjoy. There are also opportunities to integrate hands-on experiences with manipulation of phonemes using Elkonin boxes, movement, and technology. Successful and positive beginning reading experiences are essential to the development of the literacy skills necessary to becoming a skilled reader, including phonological awareness.

Reflection Questions

1. What types of systematic, explicit phonological awareness instruction are included in your current scope and sequence?

2. How do you include phonological awareness in your instruction?

3. In what ways does this chapter support the instruction you already provide?

4. What new learning have you gained about phonological awareness? What new strategies will you try?

Chapter 2

Phonics: Systematic and Explicit

From the Classroom

All abuzz, students are talking, quickly figuring out which partner will talk first. The teacher walks around the small carpet area, tracking student engagement. She hears two students simultaneously blurt, "EEEEEEE," and then more students join in until the entire class rings with the double /e/ sound.

"One, two, three, eyes on me," says the teacher.

"One, two, eyes on you." Students return to their positions as they visually track the teacher to her seat.

"Great job, friends, you are correct: double e does make the /ē/ sound. Let's try using the double e in words! Are you ready to chain?!"

With boundless energy, students sing out their version of Aretha Franklin's song: "Chain chain chain, chain chain chain!!" Franklin would be proud!

With the wave of a hand, the teacher quiets them. She pulls over the placard holder, places a double e in the middle, and adds consonants on each end to make the word *sweet*.

Squirming students thrust their hands in the air. With ease, the teacher calls on a student. "What strategy helped you figure out this word?"

"You taught us...I used my lips and Stretchy, the long *e*," a bouncy little girl replies. "Like this," she forms her mouth and makes the /sw/ sound, slowly transforming the shape of her mouth while blending the sounds. She moves her mouth again to make the double *e* sound and ends with a hard *t* sound.

Two students nod in agreement.

"Wonderful job, friend," the teacher enthusiastically replies, knowing that the systematic approach to teaching phonics skills was sticking. On to more words…

—Tyisha Brown
First Grade Teacher
Cowlishaw Elementary
Naperville, Illinois

Background Information and Research

"Mom, have you played Wordle yet today?" Robin's daughter Sophie asks as she walks in the door from school.

"Not yet," Robin answers.

Wordle, created by Josh Wardle (2021), is an internet word game phenomenon in which you have six guesses to determine a five-letter word. For every word guess entered, the computer turns the letter tile to yellow if that letter is in the word but not in the correct position in the word. The tile turns green if the letter is in the word and in the correct position. Robin and Sophie play every day and send their scores to each other. They are both competitive, but more fun than winning is how they talk about the strategies they use to figure out the word. Robin begins with the word *adieu* because it has four out of the five vowels in it. Robin feels that it gives her an advantage in determining the vowels used right away. Sophie decides to start with a word that contains the most common and most frequently used letters in the English language, *steal*. She also changes her start word sometimes. Today, the word was *skill*. It took Robin all six guesses to figure it out. The *i*, which was used correctly in the third position, did help her a bit, so for her second guess, she chose to incorporate more common consonants: *bring*. She did not get any help from that word. She went in another direction and tried *soils*. This time, s and l were in the correct positions. Robin's game board looked like this: S_IL_. She quickly figured out that the rime in the word was *ill*, but there were so many possibilities for the onset. She tried *spill*. Wrong. She tried *still*. Wrong. She was worried that this would be the first time she would not guess the word correctly in six tries. She wavered between *swill* and *skill*. *Skill* seemed more common than *swill*, so she typed it in and got it correct. Sophie got it in five tries. She said the *s* and *l* helped her more quickly and, luckily, she knew it could not be *still* because the *t* was incorrect on her first guess. Wordle only gives you one chance a day to play, so there is always tomorrow.

For many years, there has been a debate about how students best learn to read and the best way to teach students to read. That debate frequently focuses on one area in particular: phonics. The bottom line is phonics is a method of teaching reading that ensures students have the skillset to match letters or groups of letters with the sounds they represent. This letter-sound correspondence is also known as the alphabetic principle, decoding, or word recognition skills. According to leading researchers who have studied the Science of Reading for the last three decades, the need for teachers to provide explicit, systematic phonics instruction for students to become skilled readers is "settled science" (Blevins 2020; Duke and Mesmer 2018; Foorman et al. 2016; Moats 2020a; National Reading Panel 2000a).

The story above uses the words *guess* and *luckily*. Those terms are not really accurate, though, when we think about the phonics skills we are using to determine the Wordle of the day. Nell Duke (2022) is one of the first researchers to write about the connections between proficiency in letter-sound correspondence and knowledge of phonics patterns, and success in word games, such as Wordle. Duke (2022) lists five lessons we can learn from Wordle that will guide our thinking through this chapter, as we talk about phonics instruction and its importance to reading success:

- Some letters are more common than others.
- The position of letters in a word matters.
- Letters and sounds do not have a one-to-one match.
- Vocabulary knowledge is important to reading and spelling.
- Phonics and spelling can be engaging.

Connection to the Rope

Phonics is the essential element of reading. According to Gough and Tunmer's Simple View of Reading (1986), phonics is the element that contributes to students' ability to decipher the words on the page, a necessary skill to "build the reading brain" (Seidenberg 2017; Stewart n.d.; Willingham 2017). The Simple View of Reading and Scarborough's Reading Rope model (2001) provide the foundation for the evidence-based components required to develop automatic, strategic readers. When students begin to recognize letter-sound relationships in words more easily, quickly, and proficiently, it strengthens their word recognition (a strand in the Reading Rope model). This leads to increased automaticity, one of the essential areas for a skilled reader in building toward the goal of reading comprehension.

Implications for Teaching and Learning

Evidence clearly shows that teaching phonics must be an intentional component of research-based reading instruction. The debate continues within teacher circles about how to teach letter names and sounds. At the heart of the debate is the question, "Should instruction be explicit and systematic, or random and implicit?" The answer lies in the research. If phonics instruction is to best meet the needs of students, it must be *systematic* and *explicit*. Following a logically ordered scope and sequence during phonics instruction and building on the continuum of letter-sound relationships from the simple to the complex ensures that the skills needed for decoding are not left to chance. Each lesson builds on the one before it. Research reveals that the systematic and explicit teaching of phonics improves the rate at which students acquire letter-sound correspondence (National Reading Panel 2000a). Explicit phonics instruction means that the objective of the lesson is clear, focused, and intentional, with guided support and scaffolding throughout as needed. In systematic and explicit instruction, teachers directly guide students through the skills that are being learned and then assess for mastery. Teachers can identify where students have gaps and teach directly to fill in what is missing through more direct instruction and opportunities to practice the skill.

> Following a logically ordered scope and sequence during phonics instruction, building on the continuum of letter-sound relationships from the simple to the complex, ensures that the skills needed for decoding are not left to chance.

Research shows that one of the reasons explicit phonics instruction has received negative attention in the past is because it has been seen as rote, boring, and inauthentic (Blevins 2020; Duke and Mesmer 2018; Foorman et al. 2016; Moats 2020a; National Reading Panel 2000a). This does not have to be the case. Teachers can learn a lot from the conclusions drawn by Nell Duke (2022), which underscore why a game like Wordle has become so popular. When teachers use what they know about the Science of Reading to plan engaging lessons using phonics skills, students will be introduced to new learning and will remain engaged. These lessons should incorporate movement: clapping, patting, and hopping. Teachers need to incorporate repetition and rhyme using poems that contain decodable text. Learning word patterns is enjoyable for students. Engaging phonics lessons include the use of manipulatives such as Elkonin boxes and magnetic letters, and online games and apps to build words and explore patterns. During explicit instruction and practice of phonics skills, teachers should allow students to circle, highlight, and underline patterns using pencils, pens, crayons, markers, and at times, other novel writing utensils (Duke and Mesmer 2018). Moving from the letter to the word level, to phrases, to decodable text, and finally to words in context gives students purpose for reading and helps them weave their beginning word recognition skills into their beginning comprehension skills to intertwine the strands of their reading ropes closely together. Remember that each new phonics skill is unearthing more words for students to read. This uncovering of the skills to access more text is authentically engaging and empowering, especially when success is evident and students are given ample opportunities to showcase their new skills.

Key Terms for Teacher Understanding

The following chart provides definitions of essential terms educators need to know and an example of each one.

Term and Definition	Example
consonant—the following 21 letters in the alphabet: *b, c, d, f, g, h, j, k, l, m, n, p, q, r, s, t, v, w, x, y, z*; these letters represent consonant sounds that are made when air is partially blocked by the tongue, teeth, or lips when making a sound while speaking	Kristy, a first grader, is excited about her small-group reading time. She likes working with her teacher on letter-sound correspondence using the letter chart and whiteboards. They are practicing beginning consonant sounds today. Her teacher first says a sound by itself, and each person in the group takes turns pointing to the consonant on the letter chart that matches the sound. Next, the teacher shows the group a picture card, says the word the picture represents, and asks students to write the letter that makes the beginning consonant sound they hear. The first picture is *bat*. Students write the letter *b*. Kristy is happy that the teacher notices she writes the letter *b* correctly. Kristy practices a few more beginning consonant letters and sounds with the teacher before looking in her decodable text for the consonants she practiced.

Term and Definition	Example
consonant clusters—when two or more consonants are next to each other in a word and each consonant sound (phoneme) can be heard individually; the term *consonant cluster* refers to the written form, while the term *consonant blend* refers to the spoken form, but they are often used interchangeably	Ms. Williams is using Elkonin boxes during small-group reading to work on grapheme-phoneme matching with consonant blends and clusters at the beginning of words. Ms. Williams has given students the corresponding number of boxes to match the number of phonemes in each word. Students push a counter into the box as they hear the phoneme and then write the consonant cluster they hear at the beginning of the word underneath the boxes. The first word is *crab*. There are four phonemes in *crab*: /k/ /r/ /ă/ /b/, so students push four counters up one at a time into the corresponding boxes. Ms. Williams does the first word with them as a model. She then asks them to listen for the consonant blend at the beginning and write the two consonants that they hear. The consonant cluster they hear is *cr*. Ms. Williams reinforces that they hear two separate phonemes, /k/ and /r/, which are written as *cr*. Students repeat this practice with more words: *clap*, *stop*, *swim*, *flip*, *snap*, and *crib*.
decodable text—texts that contain a large percentage of words that incorporate the letter-sound relationships students have already been taught	Ms. Moore chooses a decodable text titled *A Nap* to use with her small group for practice reading words with the CVC pattern. Before they read the story, she has students read the title and look at the short vowel sound *a* in the words *cap* and *map*. She tells students that most of the words in the story will have a CVC pattern with the short vowel *a*. Students' first task with the decodable text is to circle or highlight all the words they find with this phonics pattern. Then students practice reading the text at school and at home to become fluent with CVC words that have the short vowel *a*.

(Continued)

Term and Definition	Example
digraph—two letters that make one sound; **consonant digraphs** are two consonants together that make a single sound, such as /ch/, /sh/, /ph/, /wh/, and /ck/; **vowel digraphs** are groups of two letters together that make a single sound, one of which must be a vowel	Ms. Martinez has made a T-chart for today's lesson for students to sort words where the long vowel sound *a* is represented by two different vowel digraphs, *ai* and *ay*. On the left side of the chart, she writes the vowel digraph *ay*. On the right side of the chart, she writes the vowel digraph *ai*. She holds up a picture card of a brain. Students say the word *brain*. Ms. Martinez writes the word *brain* under the *ai* side of the chart and underlines the vowel digraph *ai*. Students say the word with her. Next, she holds up a picture of a *train*. She writes the word *train* under the *ai* side of the chart. For words that are hard to represent with a picture, she uses a sentence with the word missing. For example, she asks students which words are missing in the following sentence: "Students _ _ _ _ outside during the _ _ _ at school when the sun is shining." The words are *play* and *day*, both of which she writes under the *ay* side of the chart. Other words with the long *a* vowel sound made by the vowel digraphs *ai* or *ay* sorted on the T-chart include *mail, nail, pain, rain, stain, paid, braid, pay, lay, stay, tray, may, say*, and *spray*.

Term and Definition	Example
diphthong—a new sound formed by combining two vowels in a single syllable; examples of diphthongs include *ow, ou, aw, au, oi, oy*	Jarrison, a second grader, is completing a cut-and-paste activity after learning about the diphthong *ow*. His paper is numbered from 1 to 5, and next to each number is written *ow*. At the bottom of the paper are the letters *c, cr, d, n*, and *fr*. Jarrison will cut out the letters and make five words that contain *ow*. Some letters are repeated because they will be used in more than one word. Jarrison reads the clue to figure out which letters he will glue next to the *ow* to make the correct word. The clue for number 1 says: "This is an animal on a farm that gives us milk." Jarrison cuts out the *c* and glues it down in front of the *ow* to make the word *cow*. The other words he will have to make are *crown, crowd, frown*, and *down*.

(Continued)

Term and Definition	Example
explicit—stated clearly and in detail; explicit instruction is where skills are taught directly to students through lessons with clear objectives and guided practice with scaffolded support	Mr. Hughes writes the word *cat* on the board. He tells the class that today they are going to learn how to blend sounds together to read words with the consonant-vowel-consonant (CVC) pattern using their new phonics skill, short *a*. He begins to explicitly teach: "Look at this word I wrote on the board. It has a consonant-vowel-consonant pattern, also known as CVC. Say that with me: CVC." He writes *C-V-C* underneath the letters as the children say them. "The first letter is the consonant *c*. The *c* makes the /k/ sound. The second letter is the short vowel *a*. The *a* makes the /ă/ sound. The final letter is the consonant *t*. The *t* makes the /t/ sound." He blends the sounds together as he runs his finger under each letter, and then has students chorally repeat and blend the sounds as he runs his finger under each letter again. Mr. Hughes models this explicit instruction with at least five more words: *bag, man, dad, ram,* and *cab.* He then has students work with partners and gives each pair a list of five more CVC short *a* words. They practice what he has just modeled. As he walks around, he listens in and offers support when needed.

Term and Definition	Example
implicit—suggested but not directly expressed or stated; implicit instruction is the exposure of students to ideas and concepts through opportunities for interaction with books and/or other materials	Mrs. Flores shares an engaging and funny poem she wrote, titled "Mice Are Nice." She displays the poem on chart paper and reads it aloud, encouraging students to read along with her. The poem includes a range of *i*-consonant-*e* words, including *mice, nice, bike, bite, kite, time, ride,* and *nine.* After reading the poem together several times, Mrs. Flores provides a copy of the poem to each student and asks students what they notice about the poem. Students analyze the words and discover the *i*-consonant-*e* pattern. Mrs. Flores affirms this and asks students to highlight words that fit the pattern. Rather than using direct instruction, Mrs. Flores is using an implicit instructional strategy to support phonics and word analysis skills.
morpheme—the smallest unit of meaning that cannot be further divided; the smallest meaningful part of a word; examples of types of morphemes: prefix, suffix, base, root	Jin, a second grader, is learning about morphemes. His teacher taught him that the prefix *re–* means "again." They read a poem together that includes the words *replay* (to play again) and *redo* (to do it again) to practice decoding words with *re–* and understand their meaning. Jin has a list of base words: *read, heat, joy, play, laugh,* and *fill.* He sorts the words into two columns: bases that can be made into a new word by adding *re–,* and bases that cannot be made into a new word by adding *re–.* In the first column he correctly writes the words *reread, reheat, replay,* and *refill.* He understands that these are all new words with new meanings that can be made by adding the prefix, or morpheme, *re–* to the beginning of the base word.

(Continued)

Term and Definition	Example
systematic—organized and carefully planned; systematic instruction means intentionally sequenced lessons and activities to ensure skill mastery	At the beginning of the year, Ms. Smith was given a scope and sequence that contained a systematic plan to teach phonics in her first-grade classroom. She likes how each lesson builds on the previous lesson, moving from the simple to the complex. When teaching words with letters that make short vowel sounds in a systematic way, the order of the letters in the lessons is *a, i, o, u, e*. Ms. Smith will teach the letter *a* and its corresponding short vowel *a* sound first. Her students will learn to read words with short *a* in them, such as *sat, cap,* and *ran*. They will then read sentences with words containing the short *a* sound, such as *The cat sat on the mat*. Next Ms. Smith will teach the letter *i* and its corresponding short vowel sound /ĭ/ with words such as *sit, lid,* and *him*. The sentences they practice will contain the new learning (words with short *i*) but also the previous learning (words with short *a*), such as *Kim hid jam in Matt's van*.
trigraph—a single sound that is represented by three letters; examples include *tch, sch*	Faye writes the three letters, *tch*, on the whiteboard at her desk as her teacher writes them on the chart paper in the front of the room. Her teacher underlines the three letters and says that these three letters together in a word make the sound /ch/. Faye repeats the sound /ch/ with the rest of the class. The teacher says the word *catch* as she writes it on the chart. Faye repeats the word and writes it on her whiteboard, *c-a-t-c-h*. She underlines the *tch*. Faye repeats this process with these words: *match, patch, latch, watch, pitch,* and *stitch*.

Term and Definition	Example
vowel—the following five letters: *a, e, i, o, u;* these letters represent sounds made when the air flows freely while speaking; a **short vowel** is a vowel sound that has a shorter duration of the sound being made; a **long vowel** is a vowel sound that sounds like the letter name and has a longer duration of the sound being made; the letter *y* acts as a vowel in some words, such as *my, fly,* or *cry*	Bethanie is working on distinguishing short and long vowel sounds. She and her partner Michele have a stack of picture cards, including a dog, a cat, a pig, a cup, a boat, rain, a gate, and a bike. Bethanie must choose a card and place it under the heading on the paper that says *Short Vowel Sound* or *Long Vowel Sound*. Bethanie chooses *cup* and places it under the *Short Vowel Sound* column. Michele agrees. Michele chooses *bike* and places it in the *Long Vowel Sound* column. The first graders continue to take turns placing the cards in their correct categories until the time is up. The teacher comes around to provide feedback. If students disagree, they raise their hands to ask for help. If they finish before time is up, they shuffle the cards and start over or trade cards with another group.

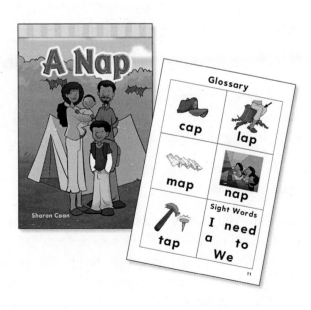

Word Reading Practice

Grades: K–1

Description

After learning the targeted phonics pattern through explicit instruction, students engage in word reading of decodable text as the next step in learning. This strategy can be used in whole-group or small-group instruction. In the example provided below, students will practice and review short vowel *i*.

Rationale

Word Reading Practice with decodable text provides students with an opportunity to practice phonics skills in context. This helps students connect the skills they practiced in isolation with the teacher to sentences they are reading in a book. Students engage in word reading of decodable text as part of this learning progression: word, sentence, text.

Process

1. Choose a decodable text with words that feature the phonics pattern you are focusing on. For example, in *Big Pig* (Coan 2012), the pattern is CVC words with a short *i* sound found in words that end in a rime with a short *i*, such as *big* and *pig*.

2. Review the text and find examples of words with the specific phonics pattern highlighted. *Big Pig* has the following four words: *big*, *pig*, *dig*, and *wig*.

3. Ask students to listen closely as you say the words, and have them share the sounds they hear in each word.

4. Write the words using the sounds on a sheet of chart paper, and show students how each word represents the phonics pattern highlighted. Sound out each letter as you write it, and underline the phonics pattern. For example, in *Big Pig*, the words above represent the short *i* vowel sound and the *ig* rime would be underlined.

5. Have students help you make a short list of other words with the phonics pattern. For example, in *Big Pig,* more short *i* rimes include these words: *frig, gig, zig, swig, twig, jig, rig,* and *fig.*

6. Write the sentences from the book on chart paper, using words with the phonics pattern for more practice. Example sentences using words from *Big Pig* include the following: *The pig is big*; *I see a wig*; and *He can jig and dig.*

7. Have students help you identify the words with the phonics pattern. Underline the words, and say each one slowly.

8. Read the sentences, and have students identify the pattern in them.

9. Discuss with students the meaning of any words they do not know. For example, the word *jig* in the final sentence of *Big Pig* is a type of dance.

10. Give each student a copy of the decodable text that contains the phonics pattern. Read the title on the cover to students as you point out the pattern in the title or first sentences of the book. As you read each page, point to each word containing the phonics pattern as you read it.

11. Have students work in groups and take turns reading pages from the story. Then have the group read the last page together. Remind students to practice using proper voice and expression as they read their pages. Ask them to switch the order to read a different set of pages.

He can dig.

7

Differentiation

- Incorporate sound into the story by having students make a noise every time they hear you read a word that has the targeted phonics pattern.

- Incorporate movement by having students move (quick dance move, stand up, etc.) every time you read a word that has the targeted phonics pattern.

- Have students make up their own sentences using the words with the targeted phonics pattern.

- Challenge students to make stories using mostly words with the targeted phonics pattern.

Flashlight Reading

Grades: K–1

Description

Students shine a flashlight on words that have the phonics pattern highlighted by the teacher.

Rationale

Flashlight Reading allows students to work on quick visual recognition of phonics patterns in words, to make connections between words with the same pattern, and to practice reading more words that incorporate the pattern in text.

Process

After providing explicit instruction on a specific phonics pattern, use this strategy to engage students in recognizing the pattern.

1. Choose a decodable text with words that include the phonics pattern you are highlighting.

2. Distribute a small flashlight to each student. Model using the flashlight by turning it on and shining the light on the pattern as you find it in words.

3. After students have practiced with you to find the pattern, continue to use this practice as you read decodable text. For example, have students point their flashlights to:

   - a word that rhymes with _____
   - a word that has a CVC pattern
   - a word that has a digraph
   - a word that has (*the phonics pattern being studied*)

Differentiation

- Make copies of a text or provide laminated copies, and have students use highlighters or dry erase markers to identify patterns as they read independently.

- Have students work with partners. Ask students to check their partner's work as they highlight or identify patterns in text.

- Challenge students to find more than one pattern or to find "rule-breakers" as they read.

Quick Find, Quick Picture, Quick Write

Grades: K–1

Description

Students find a word in a text with the phonics pattern selected by the teacher, then they draw a picture of the word to connect the meaning, and finally they write the word to practice letter-sound correspondence.

Rationale

Quick Find, Quick Picture, Quick Write incorporates a multimodal approach to reading and writing.

Process

After providing explicit instruction on a specific phonics pattern, use this strategy to engage students in recognizing the pattern.

1. Choose a decodable text with words that include the phonics pattern you are highlighting. Tell students you are going to find a word on the page with that pattern. Say, "I am looking at a word on this page. It has the ___ pattern." Point to the word.

2. On a sheet of chart paper, draw a quick picture of the word. Ask students to identify the picture by saying the word. Say, "I pointed to ___ and I drew___."

3. Next to the picture, write the word. Point to the word on the page again, and ask students if you wrote the correct word next to your picture. Have students say the word.

4. Tell students they will do this in the text they are reading. Distribute small whiteboards or sticky notes to students along with their decodable texts. As they read the first page, call out a word and ask students to point to it in the text.

5. Once they have pointed to the word, have them draw a picture of the word on their whiteboards or sticky notes. Then ask them to write the word under the picture. Continue this process through the rest of the text.

Differentiation

- Have students work with partners. Let each partner take turns choosing a word in the text, and then have their partner draw the word and write the word.

- Tell students you are looking at a word that has a specific pattern, but do not identify the word. Ask students to draw a picture of the word they think you are looking at on sticky notes and to write the word under their pictures. Check their work by having them hold up their sticky notes.

- Have students take turns leading this activity with the class.

Long Vowel Swat

Description

Students use a fly swatter to swat words that have specific long vowels.

Rationale

Long Vowel Swat provides a hands-on, tactile strategy for students to practice distinguishing the long vowel sounds and the different long vowel patterns (digraphs or clusters) that can make them.

Process

1. Make cards with a range of words that showcase a long vowel pattern. The number of cards can vary depending on the size of the group, but 25 is a good amount. Some examples of vowel patterns include:

   - long *a*—*a*, *a_e*, *ay*
   - long *e*—*e*, *e_e*, *ee*, *y* (like *baby*)
   - long *i*—*i*, *i_e*, *y_e*, *igh*, *y* (like *cry*)
   - long *o*—*o*, *o_e*, *oa*, *ow*
   - long *u*—*u*, *u_e*, *oo*, *ew*

2. Use multiple fly swatters so several students can play at one time in a large group, or have smaller groups of students play. Each student will take turns swatting a word.

3. Spread the word cards out on a table.

4. Say the vowel sound, and have students look for a word card that shows a word with that vowel sound. When they find a word, have them swat it with their fly swatter. The student must read the word aloud to keep it.

5. The student with the most words at the end wins the game.

Differentiation

This strategy can be differentiated through its difficulty of skill level.

- Start with words that only contain long vowel sounds made in the CVE pattern.

- For more scaffolding, play with cards that only represent two long vowel patterns.

- Use this strategy with any letter-sound relationship or phonics pattern that has been previously taught.

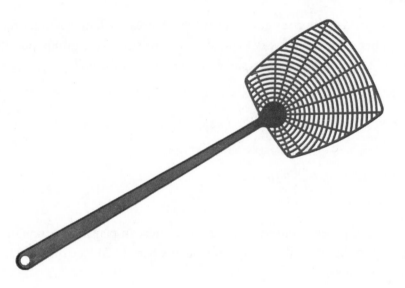

Instruction for Higher Grade Levels

Foundational phonics skills instruction for intermediate grades and students in middle and high school will likely be intervention to support gaps in knowledge. For success in teaching phonics skills to older students, begin by identifying the phonics skills missing using an assessment such as the Quick Phonics Screener (Hasbrouck 2017). When gaps in knowledge are identified, create a sequence for instruction. Provide explicit, systematic instruction individually or in small groups as needed. It is imperative that older students receive instruction that is research-based. Explicit instruction should be used in the upper grades. Some examples include movement, letter-sound sentence recognition within text, and hands-on manipulation of words, word parts, and patterns. (More on phonics instruction in upper grades and with multisyllabic words can be found in Chapter 3: Beyond Foundational Phonics, pages 73–92.)

Moving Forward: Top Must-Dos

Phonics lessons and activities should be carefully planned, purposeful, and engaging. They should be implemented through at least third grade in daily whole-group lessons, following a research-based scope and sequence. Lessons can also be delivered in small groups or individually to meet student needs.

Teach Letter-Sound Correspondence Systematically

Just as research shows the value of teaching phonological awareness using a systematic scope and sequence, research also supports that letter-sound correspondence must be taught explicitly and sequentially to develop skilled readers. Experts agree that instruction should build from students understanding the alphabetic principle (e.g., that words are made up of letters that represent sounds), to students generating and blending those sounds as they recognize patterns, to greater automaticity of word recognition in the goal of becoming fluent readers (Ehri et al. 2001; Kilpatrick 2015, 2016; Moats 2020a; Scarborough 2001). Think of this continuum in levels, building from recognizing a letter, then a sound, then a word, then a phrase, and then moving into decodable text and reading in context.

When creating a scope and sequence that focuses on foundational phonics skills, remember:

- Provide explicit instruction.
- Build lessons from the simple to the complex.
- Sequence skills based on the research-based phonics continuum of learning: letter, sound, word, phrase, decodable text.
- Connect new learning to previous knowledge.
- Provide feedback frequently through progress monitoring.
- Scaffold instruction, reteach, and review when needed.

Teach Word Structure

Examining the structure of a word and figuring out its parts quickly helps lessen the difficulty of reading for some students. Students do not do this naturally, but when taught to look carefully at words and notice patterns through explicit instruction, they will start to make connections as they read new words. Linnea C. Ehri (1995, 2014), a leading researcher on word recognition, details her four phases of word-reading development that lead up to examining the structures of words. The first three phases are:

- the prealphabetic phase, where there is no letter-sound correspondence and children recognize words based on visual cues;
- the partial alphabetic phase, where readers use some letters of the alphabet and try to pronounce words, especially using the beginning or ending sounds; and
- the full alphabetic phase, which includes phoneme-grapheme mapping and the recognition of sight words.

The consolidated alphabetic phase is the final of Ehri's four phases of word reading development (1995, 2014). In this phase, students develop automaticity through deeper understanding of word structure, word families, morphemes, orthographic mapping, and syllable patterns. The implication for teachers is that during explicit instruction of new phonics patterns, lists of words containing the pattern must be generated. The pattern must be circled, underlined, or highlighted. Students should practice writing the pattern in words and then finding words with the pattern in the reading they are doing with the teacher during whole-group instruction or through practice with decodable text.

Provide Practice Decoding at the Word, Phrase, and Text Levels

As students begin to understand letter-sound relationships and increase their knowledge of letter patterns, they are quicker to figure out new words they encounter. This ability to use letter-sound correspondence to recognize words is known as *decoding*. After teachers provide direct instruction on the phonics skill to students, they must provide opportunities to practice the skill. This practice begins at the word level. For example:

- Teachers model the pattern explicitly with the word in isolation first.

- Students make a connection between the written pattern and the sound the pattern makes. For example, the word *lake* follows a vowel-consonant-silent e (VCE) pattern. The vowel makes a long *a* sound.

- The teacher provides opportunities to practice decoding more VCE words with different long vowels.

- As students begin to master decoding VCE at the word level, they start to practice with phrases that include VCE words. The phrase can include a word with a pattern already mastered such as CVC and any learned sight words, such as *the big lake* or *a hot cake*. These opportunities for practice are still in isolation but can be paired with pictures or word hunts around the room.

The next phase of decoding practice is at the text level with the words in context. Decodable readers provide a scaffold for students learning to move between reading words in isolation to authentic text. They allow students to focus on mastery of the letter-sound relationship while increasing automaticity within the context of sentences.

Further Considerations

Embed Phonics Mini-Lessons in Whole-Group and Small-Group Learning

Both whole-group and small-group learning formats can be effective in the teaching and reinforcement of phonics mini-lessons, so all students should be engaged in daily, explicit phonics instruction in either or both of these formats. The role of the teacher, the level of support needed by students, and the resources and materials being used in the lesson can be determining factors in whether a lesson works better in a large or small group. The use of regular assessment will support decision-making as you plan for phonics instruction. Quick formative-assessment checks can help you determine what instruction students need next. Most new phonics skill lessons can be introduced to the group as a whole, and students can turn and talk to their partners or table groups to brainstorm and add to the conversation as they learn. For intervention or to provide more intense, personalized feedback with a student who is struggling with a concept, a smaller group, or even one-on-one instruction might be necessary. If a teacher has limited manipulatives for students to use to practice a strategy, then students in small groups can take turns.

Beware of Haphazard Scope and Sequencing

Embedding explicit phonics skills into your teaching does not require a lot of time each day, but it must be organized, planned, and systematic to have the most impact. When phonics skills are taught out of sequence, students can become easily confused. Nell Duke and Heidi Anne Mesmer emphasize that two important components of beginning reading instruction in phonics are that enough time is spent on explicit instruction and that teachers must know what to teach and how to teach it, which means having a well-designed scope and sequence (2018). Duke and Mesmer go on to say that when phonics instruction is not logically sequenced, information is missed. They illustrate this point by discussing the idea of students organizing the connections they make between phonics skills and patterns in words in cognitive "file folders." These folders become grouped in students' brains and are more easily accessed as new information and learning is added (2018). If patterns are not connected or the lesson sequence does not make sense, it makes word recognition and automaticity more difficult. There are numerous resources for research-based phonics scope and sequences. Using the foundational standards will provide you a base for understanding the skills students need to develop. In addition, you can turn to curriculum that is based on the standards and the research on effective phonics instruction.

My Teaching Checklist

Are you ready to develop students' phonics skills so they may be successful readers? Use this checklist to help you get started!

Phonics: Systematic and Explicit

Look Fors	Description
Students have consistent access to instruction and letter-sound learning.	• Use a daily scope and sequence with logically sequenced skills progressing from simple to complex. • Include explicit direct teaching opportunities with clear objectives and modeling. • Build time to review and reteach into the scope and sequence. • Provide small-group or individualized instruction for students who are struggling with skills.
Students have multiple opportunities to practice phonics skills.	• Explicitly teach whole-group phonics lessons daily. • Provide small-group lessons for students to practice skills. • Provide students with decodable text for use at school and at home. • Provide students with time to read and practice their skills. • Incorporate games for practice. • Ensure reading and writing tasks use the skills learned.

Chapter Summary

Phonics is an essential element in the teaching of reading as well as a foundational literacy skill. Phonics instruction provides students with the structures that lead to increased automaticity in word recognition, laying the foundation to become more proficient readers. Due to the importance of understanding letter-sound relationships in decoding, increased word recognition, and reading achievement, phonics instruction must be systematic and explicit. Further, this instruction must include multiple built-in opportunities to assess, reteach, and continuously scaffold and review skills both in isolation and in context through reading and writing.

Reflection Questions

1. How do you include phonics instruction during the day?

2. In what ways does this chapter support the instruction you already provide?

3. What teacher and student resources do you have for phonics instruction?

4. What new learning have you gained about phonics? What new strategies will you try?

Chapter 3

Beyond Foundational Phonics: Multisyllabic Words and More

Background Information and Research

Phonics instruction should continue after the primary grades. Once students learn the foundational phonics skills discussed in Chapter 2, including letter-sound correspondence, blending, deleting, manipulating letters and sounds, and decoding, the attention in older grades moves to using knowledge of syllable types to decode multisyllabic words, and to morphology, which is the study of words and their parts. As students discover more about how words work, they begin to decode and read words more fluently. Through morphology, they learn the meanings of word parts. Students can then use this knowledge when reading to break words apart and decipher their meanings. They learn their etymology, or origin, which leads to a greater interest in and understanding of how words are connected and build on each other through similarities in individual parts, such as roots and affixes (see Key Terms for Teacher Understanding on page 76).

Connection to the Rope

Scarborough's Reading Rope model (2001), one of the key models supporting the framework of evidence-based components leading to the development of skilled readers, identifies *decoding* as part of the word recognition strand. Decoding skills, or the ability to pronounce words by applying letter-sound correspondence, are expanded during the reading of multisyllabic words by learning how to break apart words into smaller syllables or sections, understanding the meaning of those smaller word parts, and then making connections to other words with similar parts. This study of word parts and their meanings is known as *morphology* and develops students' morphological awareness (see Key Terms for Teacher Understanding on page 76).

Implications for Teaching and Learning

A common belief is that there is a point in teaching reading when students transition from learning to read to reading to learn. Teachers who subscribe to that outdated and erroneous adage often stop explicit decoding instruction because they feel students understand foundational phonics skills. But this does not hold true because in third grade and beyond, students will encounter more multisyllabic words that they will not be able to decode quickly, nor can they comprehend the meaning. William Nagy and Richard Anderson (1984) found in their research that from fifth grade on, the average students encounter approximately 10,000 new words each year that they have not previously encountered in print. These are typically content words that, if not read and understood, impact a student's ability to comprehend a text.

> To expand students' ability to engage in decoding multisyllabic words and increase morphological awareness, students must be given multiple opportunities to read daily from a variety of texts.

One of the most powerful ways to support students as they encounter more multisyllabic words in text is to ensure they know the types of syllables and how to navigate them. The six syllable types commonly recognized are open syllables, closed syllables, vowel-consonant-*e* syllables, vowel team syllables, vowel-*r* syllables, and consonant-*le* syllables. Being familiar with syllable conventions provides students with one way to decode multisyllabic words in text.

Morphology instruction supports decoding text and understanding the meanings of words through explicitly teaching word parts and their meanings. Timothy Rasinski, Nancy Padak, Rick Newton, and Evangeline Newton, authors of resources on vocabulary and morphological awareness, share important principles for teachers to be aware of when explicitly teaching skills to upper-grade students and more advanced readers. They reinforce the idea that students must connect their knowledge of existing words and word parts to words that are new and unfamiliar in order to learn the words and be able to read them more fluently (2019, 2020). This means that teachers must allow students to discuss their background knowledge of the word parts and then engage in activities that reinforce the connections between what they know and what they do not know when they learn new roots and affixes. To expand students' abilities to engage in decoding multisyllabic words and increase morphological awareness, researchers agree that students must be given multiple opportunities to read daily from a variety of texts (Duke and Mesmer 2018; Nagy and Anderson 1984; Rasinski et al. 2019, 2020).

Researchers also stress that instruction at all levels must be fun and engaging so that students learn to "play" with words and become more confident with reading multisyllabic words. Nell Duke, in her article about the game Wordle (discussed in Chapter 2), reminds teachers that having a large vocabulary gives players a greater chance to guess the word in under six tries. Having a bank of words in our memory gives us access to more options to try. Duke reiterates that "explicit teaching of meaningful word parts (morphology) supports spelling development. Similarly, vocabulary knowledge helps us to read words" (2022, para. 10). This greater word recognition will in turn help readers monitor comprehension and become more strategic and fluent readers, which is the ultimate goal of reading instruction.

> Researchers also stress that instruction at all levels must be fun and engaging so that students learn to "play" with words and become more confident with reading multisyllabic words.

Key Terms for Teacher Understanding

The following chart provides definitions of essential terms educators need to know and an example of each one. Since terminology varies, many of the definitions here are based on the work of vocabulary experts Timothy Rasinski, Nancy Padak, Rick Newton, and Evangeline Newton (2019, 2020).

Term and Definition	Example
affix—any word part that attaches to the beginning or end of a word; an umbrella term for prefixes and suffixes	Mia is working on a matching activity to help her understand how adding affixes (prefixes and suffixes) to base words can change their meaning. She has a list of bases: *smile, laugh, jump, pack, break, sing, play, brown*, and *connect*. She also has a list of prefixes (*un–, re–, dis–*) and a list of suffixes (*–er, –s, –ing, –ed, –ish, –able*). There are multiple combinations of words that can be made by matching these base words with the affixes, so first Mia can match any word with any affix to make a new word. Examples of possible combinations: • smile = *smiling, smiled, smiles* • jump = *jumper, jumped, jumping, jumps* • connect = *connected, reconnect, disconnect, connecting* • brown = *brownish, browned, browning, browner, browns* The ultimate challenge for Mia is to see if she can correctly match each base word to one affix to make a new word without repeating any of the affixes. She writes these words: *smiled, laughing, jumps, singer, brownish, breakable, disconnect, replay*, and *unpack*.

Term and Definition	Example
base—a root that carries the basic meaning of a word; a base may be a word part or a stand-alone word; some use the terms *base* and *root* interchangeably	Mr. McShane is working with a small group on identifying the base of a word. Each student has a small whiteboard and a marker. Mr. McShane writes the word *playing* on his board. He uses the word in a sentence: "The boy is playing outside with his dogs." He then underlines the base word, *play*. He uses *play* in a sentence: "The boy wants to play with his dogs outside." Then he writes *play + ing = playing*, and reminds students that when you add a suffix or a prefix to a base word, it changes the meaning and the way you use the word. Students write the next word on their own whiteboards: *rewind*. Each student underlines the base and shows Mr. McShane their board. The base of *rewind* is *wind*. Students take turns using *wind* and *rewind* in sentences: "We need to rewind the ribbon back onto its spool;" "Wind that string up into a ball." Mr. McShane uses other words to practice underlining the bases: *cat*s, *jump*ed, un*box*, *fear*less, *fold*able, en*joy*, and *bounc*y.

(Continued)

Term and Definition	Example
compound words— words that are created when two or more individual words are joined together to make a new word with a new meaning; there are three types of compound words: **closed compound words** (*football, butterfly, cowboy*), **open compound words** (*living room, coffee table, ice cream*), and **hyphenated compound words** (*merry-go-round, part-time*)	Ms. Culmo is teaching a lesson on the most common type of compound words, closed compound words. She places a picture of a rainbow on chart paper. She writes the word underneath the picture, keeping a space between the words *rain* and *bow*. She explains, "*Rainbow* is a compound word. It is a new word made from two words that are joined together. Say the word with me." The students say the word. Ms. Culmo then models with the pictures and words that make the following compound words: *cowboy, barefoot, doorbell, goldfish,* and *airplane*.
etymology—the study of word origins and how meanings have evolved and changed over time	Mrs. Scott introduces a Latin base to her sixth-grade students, writing *ven, vent,* and *veni* on the board. She says, "These root words come from Latin. *Venire* and *ventus* mean 'to come.'" The students read a short story about a comic book *convention* and discuss the *event*. Learning the etymology of words supports her students in developing a complete understanding of them.

Term and Definition	Example
morphology—the study of words and their parts, how words are formed, and how they relate to other words; morphology includes studying morphemes (the smallest unit of meaning that cannot be further divided)	Carmen is writing a narrative about when she learned to play basketball. She created a first draft and is now conferencing with her teacher. Miss Kwan notices that Carmen has written her first draft in present tense. She reminds Carmen of the morphology lesson they had last week on adding the suffix *–ed* to base words to make them show past tense. Miss Kwan and Carmen review words in the draft that can be changed from present tense to past tense: *jump* to *jumped*, *dribble* to *dribbled*, and *bounce* to *bounced*. Carmen then notices *play* and changes it to *played*.
multisyllabic words—words with more than one syllable	Even though Ms. Davis teaches fourth grade, she likes to work on syllable lessons using phonological awareness first before moving on to phonics activities with multisyllabic words. During the first week of school, she has students clap their names to hear the syllables. For example, *Davis* has two syllables: Da/vis. *James* has one syllable. *Jennifer* has three syllables: Jen/ni/fer. Ms. Davis makes a chart with all students' names. She sorts them into three columns: One-syllable, Two-syllable, or Three-syllable. Ms. Davis has found that students may have done this activity with their first names but have not done this with their last names. So, to extend her introductory lessons on multisyllabic words, she also has students clap each other's last names and then add them to their chart under the appropriate columns. John/son has two syllables; Mont/gom/er/y has four syllables; Rod/ri/guez has three syllables; Wash/ing/ton has three syllables. Ms. Davis writes multisyllabic words at the top of each column as a reminder to her class that these are words with more than one syllable.

(Continued)

Term and Definition	Example
prefix—a root attached to the beginning of a word; generally, a prefix gives a word direction, negates a word with the meaning "not," or intensifies a word's meaning by adding the notion of "very"	Ms. Mason has been teaching prefixes, examples of prefixes, and their meanings all week. Julius has a chart in his journal that he made while following along with Ms. Mason. There are three sections: prefix, meaning, and example word. His chart from the week looks like this:

re–	back or again	*redone*
un–	not	*unwrap*
pre–	before	*pretest*
non–	not	*nonsense*
dis–	not or opposite of	*disbelief*
mis–	wrong or bad	*misbehave*

During reading time, Ms. Mason wants students to work at their desks and search in the books they are reading for as many words as they can find that have these prefixes, and add the words to their lists in their journals. Julius's goal is to find at least one word for each prefix. He ends up finding a lot of words for *re–* and *un–* but not as many for the others. He adds these words to his list:

- *re–: redo, regain, rebook, reform*
- *un–: unhappy, unpack, untie, undo, unfriendly*
- *pre–: premade*
- *non–: nondairy*
- *dis–: disappear*
- *mis–: misread*

Term and Definition	Example
suffix—a root attached to the end of a word; generally, a suffix changes a word's meaning and/or part of speech	José and Audriana are working together as partners. Their teacher is asking them to make word webs to practice adding suffixes to base words. Mrs. Faizan gives them a base word, and they have two minutes to add as many suffixes as they can to the base word to make new words. They can use their notes from the suffix lessons they had during the week. They can also use words they find in books or their own writing. The first word is *walk*. They write *walk* in the middle of their paper and draw a circle around it. When Mrs. Faizan says "Go!" they begin making new words by adding different suffixes to the word *walk*. When Mrs. Faizan calls "Time!" they have made the words: *walks*, *walked*, *walking*, *walker*, and *walkable*. The next word Mrs. Faizan gives them is *soft*. They have trouble at first and can only think of *softer*, so Mrs. Faizan gives them a hint to help: "How do you pet your kitten?" That helps, and they add *softly* to their list. Other words they practice include: • call: *calls*, *called*, *caller*, *calling* • care: *caring*, *careless*, *careful*, *cared* • wonder: *wonders*, *wondered*, *wondering*, *wonderer*, *wonderment*, *wonderful*

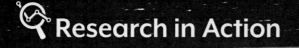

Word Analysis Skills

Grades: 2–3

Description

This strategy asks students to break an unknown word into its smaller parts, understand the meaning of each part on its own, and then put the parts back together to understand the whole word. There are multiple ways to analyze words through listening and speaking, using materials to cut apart or manipulate parts of words, or using colors or symbols to deconstruct words or identify multiple parts of words, such as the roots.

Rationale

Students need the skills to analyze multisyllabic words while reading. This strategy provides students with opportunities to practice breaking words into parts in engaging ways. As students become more proficient at quickly decoding and analyzing the parts of words, they become more fluent readers. Knowing parts of words and their meanings also helps students make connections to other words with the same parts, even if a word is unfamiliar to them.

Process

1. Have different-color markers available for this activity, to differentiate vowels from consonants. Break words into syllables and write each syllable on a magnet, a laminated card, or a sticky note so it can be moved and manipulated easily.

2. Choose a multisyllabic word to display on the board or on a sheet of chart paper. Circle the vowels in one color. For example, in the word *lesson*, circle the *e* and the *o* in blue.

3. Underline the consonants in green. In *lesson*, the *l*, *s*, *s*, and *n* would be underlined.

4. Model how to code each syllable to identify the consonant-vowel pattern. For example, in *lesson*, the code would be consonant-vowel-consonant (CVC/CVC) for both syllables. Break the word apart to show how *les/son* would be divided into syllables between the *s* and *s*.

5. Provide word cards to students, and have them work with partners to color code vowels and consonants or to code and break apart the syllables. Students can use scissors to cut the cards, or they can write the words on individual whiteboards.

6. Teach students this alternate way to analyze multisyllabic words.

   - Circle parts of the word you know: roots, affixes (prefixes/suffixes), or any other familiar word parts. For example, in the word *uneventful*, *un–*, *event*, and *–ful* would each be separately circled and identified as a prefix (*un–*), a base (*event*), and a suffix (*–ful).*

   - Say each part of the word slowly. Then say each part quickly. Blend the parts together to make a word.

   - Read a full sentence with the multisyllabic word to ensure it makes sense.

Differentiation

Students should be engaged in practicing word analysis skills and strategies individually, in pairs, or in small groups. A student's ability to analyze a word will depend on their mastery of the foundational phonics skills discussed in Chapter 2.

- Encourage hands-on manipulation of word parts for students who need more kinesthetic practice before moving to only paper and pencil. For example, use scissors to cut multisyllabic words apart.

- Color-code and/or sort words by number of syllables or by syllable patterns.

- Color-code, sort, and/or mix-and-match words using their roots, prefixes, and suffixes.

- Use magnetic letters or letter and word game tiles to create multisyllabic words.

Research in Action

- Have students hold up cards with root words, prefixes, and suffixes written on them. Incorporate movement by having students find partners to make words.

- Use technology and media such as closed captioning, graphics of words and word parts, and reference tools like an online or visual thesaurus or dictionary to help with word analysis.

- Incorporate other subject areas by having students create glossaries of words with prefixes and suffixes that they find in social studies, science, and mathematics texts.

- Have students become detectives and search for multisyllabic words or matching word parts. Gather clues using one word part (such as a prefix) to help them find other similar parts. Go on word hunts in books or magazines, print or text they find around the school, or their own writing.

Syllable Support

Grades: 2+

Description

Students learn the various syllable types to support decoding of multisyllabic words. Each type of syllable is introduced to students and taught using an explicit, systematic approach. Figure 3.1 shows the syllable types in the order they should be taught.

Rationale

Multisyllabic words present challenges for many students. Ensuring that all students understand how syllables typically function in words supports their ability to decode words. Each syllable type is unique and should be taught to students separately.

Process

1. Identify the syllable type you will be teaching. See figure 3.1.

2. Explicitly teach the syllable type. Show a word and the breakdown of the syllable. For example, display the word *barn* and say, "This word has a vowel-*r* syllable, and we know this because the vowel is followed directly by the consonant *r*."

3. Continue with several single-syllable words such as *barge*, *for*, and *stir*. Next add multisyllabic words, such as *party*, *forget*, and *stirrup*.

4. Display a list of words so everyone can see them, and practice reading and breaking the words apart.

5. Provide students with additional practice opportunities, including reading and writing independently. Students can practice reading the words in context. This should start at the word level and go to phrases, and then texts that include words with the syllable type.

6. Students should also have opportunities to practice writing the words. While you read the words aloud, students can apply the syllabication rule and write the words.

Differentiation

- When working with multisyllabic words, use different colors to show the various syllable types.

- Provide chenille stems or toothpicks for students to use to physically separate syllables in multisyllabic words.

Figure 3.1—Syllable Types

Syllable Type	Description	Examples
Closed	<ul><li>the most common type in the English language</li><li>has a short vowel followed by one or more consonants</li></ul>	*cat* *bug* *nap/kin* *ten/nis*
Vowel-Consonant-*e* (VCE)	<ul><li>the vowel is long</li><li>the syllable contains a single vowel, followed by a single consonant, and a silent *e*</li><li>commonly called the "magic *e*" syllable</li></ul>	*cake* *tide* *mope* *rude*
Open	<ul><li>the vowel is long</li><li>the syllable ends with one vowel</li><li>a consonant does not close the syllable</li></ul>	*mo/tel* *ri/val* *me*

Syllable Type	Description	Examples
Vowel team	• usually two or more vowels next to each other • represent short, long, or diphthong vowel sounds • some vowel teams include consonants (examples: *ay*, *igh*, *ow*)	*meat* *road* *bright* *say* *now*
Vowel-*r*	• the vowel is followed by the consonant *r*	*barge* *firm* *mirror* *worth* *burner*
Consonant-*le*	• *le* follows a consonant • commonly called a stable syllable	*ca/ble* *whis/tle* *bot/tle* *pud/dle*

Root Word Riddles

Grades: 4–5

Description

Root Word Riddles engage students in word play, inviting them to create and figure out riddles about words with the same root. Students guess the word by connecting clues. This activity works well for pairs of students or teams.

Rationale

Root Word Riddles is a strategy from *Building Vocabulary with Greek and Latin Roots* (Rasinski et al. 2020, 94–95). This is a fun way to get students to play with roots, be word detectives, and discover meanings of affixes on their own. Students are more likely to remember word parts and their meanings when they have practice manipulating them in authentic and contextual ways.

Process

1. Create a list of words that contain the same root, for example, *terra*. Begin by reviewing the meaning of the root: *terra* means "earth." Sample words include *terrier, terrestrial, territory, terra-cotta, terrain*, and *subterranean*. Read the list of words together. Ask students to explain what each word means. Ask how their explanations include the meaning of the root.

2. If students have not created riddles before, share some riddles with them. Spend some time solving riddles and discussing how riddles are constructed. Explain that a riddle is a series of questions designed to give clues about the answer. Ask students what kinds of clues seem particularly helpful.

3. Tell students you are going to create a riddle about one of the words in the list. They will get three clues to figure out the word. Write the first clue, which will be the definition of the word. Write "My meaning is…" (e.g., for the word *invisible*, write the following: *My meaning is "something you cannot see."*).

4. Write a second and third clue (e.g., *My opposite is visible. I have four syllables.*). End with the question, "What am I?" Have students try to guess the word.

5. Ask students to work with partners. Each pair of students chooses a word from the list and makes their own riddles to share with the class.

6. Finally, spend some time swapping riddles. When students have written riddles about the same word, point out the variety of clues and ways in which the word can be described.

Differentiation

- Students can make riddle books, perhaps by root or by word part (e.g., "Our Riddle Book of Prefixes"). These books can be added to the classroom library.

- Provide extra time or more opportunities to work with partners to scaffold this activity.

- Have students take their riddles home for family members to solve.

- Older students can make riddles for younger students and share them via school mail or email.

Word Sorts

Secondary Grades

Description

Word Sorts allow students to practice identifying similarities and differences within words. For example, students may sort words based on:

- number of syllables
- parts of words
- syllable-division patterns
- affixes
- meaning

Rationale

Word Sorts provide students the opportunity to use a range of skills that showcase their understanding of how words work. The sorts can directly correlate to specific instruction students have received in word work.

Process

1. Identify a word list that correlates to the instruction students have received in word analysis skills.

2. Model how to sort the words in a range of different ways, for example, based on different word parts such as prefix, suffix, root, or syllables.

3. Have students work with partners to sort the words. Allow them to sort words using the open-sort method, where students can select the number of categories and the category headings.

4. Ask students to share the categories they created and to explain why they made those choices. Provide time for students to explore and ask questions about other students' sorting.

5. Allow students to revisit their sorting and make adjustments if they want.

6. Provide opportunities for students to share and discuss the strategies they used to sort the word list.

Differentiation

- Students can use sorts to support the discovery of word meanings.
- Use meaning to further articulate similarities and differences between words and as sorting categories.
- Give students pictures to support understanding of words.
- Use closed sorts, where the categories are identified, for students who need additional support in sorting their words.

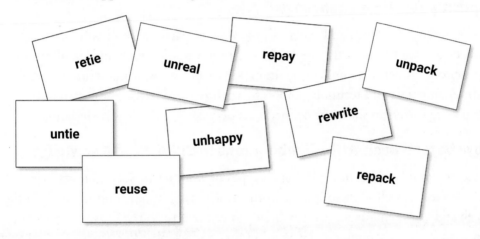

re_____	un_____

Moving Forward: Top Must-Dos

Morphological awareness lessons and phonics activities incorporating multisyllabic words, roots, and affixes should be carefully planned, purposeful, and engaging. They should be implemented in daily whole-group lessons as well as delivered in small groups or individually to meet student needs.

Provide Ample Opportunities for Word Analysis

Students must be explicitly taught strategies to analyze words and break words into their meaningful parts. Then, they must be given time and opportunity to practice this skill with words that contain familiar roots and new roots so that they can make connections between what they already know and what is unknown.

Explicitly Teach How Language Works

The etymology of words and the meaning of word parts and how words are connected must be explicitly taught daily through whole-group and small-group instruction. Students should engage in making word webs, using writing utensils of different colors and technology tools to analyze word parts. Have them use graphic organizers to show the connections between words they are learning.

Move beyond Basic Affix Combinations to Build Word Knowledge

Students should engage in exploring all types of word parts, such as roots, bases, and prefixes, as well as the origin of words, since many of our roots come from the Greek and Latin languages. This will empower them to search for word parts they know when they encounter a new word in text and use that knowledge to read and understand the meaning of the word.

Further Considerations

Recognize the Power in Morphology

Rasinski et al. (2019, 2020) emphasize the importance of morphological awareness when building on foundational phonics knowledge. The base of the word provides the core meaning, so to understand the word's morphology, students must break the word apart into its meaningful units, such as the prefix, the base, and the suffix. If students have been working with word origin and knowledge of roots in words, the meaning of a base can be identified more easily. Then the meaning of the prefix or suffix is considered, which allows students the ability to pronounce the word and to understand the meaning of the word. This morphological awareness and strategy for analyzing new words will help students with words they encounter in their daily reading in academic contexts.

My Teaching Checklist

Are you ready to develop students' skills with multisyllabic words and word roots so they may be strategic readers? Use this checklist to help you get started!

Phonics

Look Fors	Description
Students have consistent access to instruction on multisyllabic words, roots, and affixes.	• Schedule time each day for students to explicitly learn and practice new words and word parts. • Have students discover and work with new words and word parts through exposure to a variety of texts and media, including books, graphics, websites, and so on. • Plan lessons that include active engagement strategies to help students understand word parts, their meanings, and their connection to other words. • Encourage students to make personal connections with words to help them build on what they already know and transfer that knowledge to new words they encounter. • Provide small-group instruction for students who are struggling with foundational skills. Extend it to build morphological awareness with multisyllabic words.

(Continued)

My Teaching Checklist *(cont.)*

Phonics

Look Fors	Description
Students have multiple opportunities to practice morphological awareness, incorporating multisyllabic words, roots, and affixes.	• Explicitly teach whole-group lessons daily. • Provide small-group lessons for students to practice skills. • Provide students with a variety of texts and multimedia for in-context practice. • Provide students with time at school to read and practice their skills. • Incorporate games for practice. • Ensure reading and writing tasks use the skills learned.

Chapter Summary

Phonics instruction does not stop with foundational phonics skills taught during the early grades. Systematic, explicit instruction with multisyllabic words, roots, and affixes is essential to expanding students' word recognition skills and building a large vocabulary where students attach meaning to word parts (morphology) and become more strategic readers.

Reflection Questions

1. What types of instruction with multisyllabic words, roots, and affixes are included in your current scope and sequence?

2. How do you include morphological awareness instruction during the day?

3. In what ways does this chapter support the instruction you already provide?

4. What new learning have you gained about phonics instruction beyond the foundational skill level? What new strategies will you try?

Chapter 4

Sight Recognition: Familiar Words

From the Classroom

Ms. Lopez is all set up for small-group instruction during reading time today in first grade. She is working on building sight words with a group of five students to reinforce their proficiency with letter-sound correspondence. During a whole-class lesson earlier in the day, students were introduced to the words through explicit instruction.

Ms. Lopez has a whiteboard for each student and magnetic letters that students can use to form words. Students gather around the horseshoe-shaped table and wait for instructions. Ms. Lopez tells them that they are going to practice reading and spelling words they will see in the book they are reading today. The first word she says is *you*. She uses the word in a sentence: *You are my best friend.* She writes the word on her whiteboard and then asks the students to form the word on their whiteboards using the magnetic letters.

After she checks each student's board, she has the students say the letters out loud and review the letter-sound correspondence they know. With the word *you*, most recognize the initial sound /y/ and the long vowel sound *u*. Ms. Lopez asks the students to close their eyes, and when they do, she removes the *y* from each of their boards so they will only see *ou* on their boards. When they open their eyes, she asks them what letter is missing from *you*. They easily identify the missing *y* and return it to the board. She has them close their eyes again and this time removes the *o*, so that when they open their eyes, they see *y_u*. This one takes them a bit longer because of the the irregular vowel in the word, but eventually they find it. To continue building their skills, the next time she has them close their eyes, she removes different letters from each of their boards, including two letters from the student who seems to be understanding at a quicker pace.

She will practice this strategy of building sight words with small groups all week, eventually including all the high-frequency words they practiced as a whole group. These frequent opportunities to practice orthographic mapping of high-frequency words and irregular words will help students learn them as sight words that can be read with ease.

Background Information and Research

There is a persistent misconception held by many educators of what sight words are and how they should be taught. This misconception identifies sight words as a list of words that must be learned using a rote memorization technique that usually consists of "skill and drill" practice, or repeatedly reading the words written on flash cards. A thorough review of recent research supporting high-quality instruction in reading shows that sight words are more clearly defined as words students can read by sight, automatically from memory, without needing to decode them. These words include, but are not limited to, high-frequency or irregularly spelled words (Duke and Mesmer 2018; Ehri 1995, 1998, 2014; Kilpatrick 2015, 2016, 2019).

Connection to the Rope

Sight recognition of familiar words is one of the main components under the word recognition strand of Scarborough's Reading Rope model (2001), the basis for our framework of evidence-based components that lead to the development of skilled readers. This model recognizes that sight-word recognition is foundational to fluent reading. According to Really Great Reading, "Literate adults have a sight word memory of 30,000 to 70,000 words" (n.d.-b, para. 7). The explicit and systematic teaching of phonological awareness, phonemic awareness, and foundational phonics skills to early readers is what scaffolds the building of a library of sight words in adults who are strategic readers.

Implications for Teaching and Learning

Research supports that there are three areas, or stages, of reading development that all work together: phonology (pronunciation), morphology (meaning), and orthography (spelling). For a reader to become more capable, they must be proficient in the understanding of the alphabetic principle and have a large sight-word vocabulary, allowing them to recognize words quickly and accurately. Knowing the studies and reports from teachers in the classroom, leading reading researchers Duke and Mesmer (2018) warn against the rote memorization approach, where sight words are taught using only the visual identification of the letters. Making connections using letter-sound correspondences, foundational phonics skills, and relationships between words that are known to the reader leads to the ability to read words that are unknown. When working with high frequency and irregular words, teachers need to spend additional time providing explicit and systematic instruction to reinforce their storage in long-term memory.

> The more automaticity a reader has, the less time they spend on the cognitive processes of decoding words and the more time they can spend on comprehension and meaning.

As students progress as readers, there will be times when they are dependent on decoding, and other times when they are reading words with little effort. The more automaticity a reader has, the less time they spend on the cognitive processes of decoding words and the more time they can spend on comprehension and meaning (Duke and Mesmer 2018; Ehri 1995, 1998, 2014; Kilpatrick 2015, 2016, 2019). The skills that teachers must focus on to create more advanced readers with a larger sight-word vocabulary are phonological awareness, letter-sound skills, and word study.

Key Terms for Teacher Understanding

This section provides definitions of essential terms educators need to know and examples.

Terms for Words

Sight words, high-frequency words, and irregular words are related terms that can be confusing and incorrectly interchanged. The following table clarifies the differences in each term.

Term and Definition	Example
sight words—words that can be read automatically, quickly, and with little effort	Mrs. Zamora has noticed that her students are struggling with reading the **irregular words** *was*, *they*, and *said*. She realizes that these are **high-frequency words** that students see in many of the books they are beginning to read, including the decodable book they will practice reading this week. First, Mrs. Zamora writes these three words on the board and asks students which letters and sounds are familiar to them. She knows that if students can decode parts of the word, it will make it easier for them to remember the parts of the word that are not easily decodable, so she tells students that looking for patterns they know will help them with words that are irregular, like these three.
high-frequency words—words that are most used in the English language	
irregular words—words that do not follow common letter-sound correspondences or phonics patterns and are not easily decodable	Eli says he recognizes that *they* starts with the /th/ sound, a digraph they learned a few weeks ago. Mrs. Zamora applauds this answer, and the class quickly brainstorms other words they know that also start with *th*, such as *this*, *that*, *thin*, and *thick*; she lists them on the board. She then explicitly teaches students that *ey* makes the long *a* sound. She writes the sentence, "They like to skate." *(Continued)*

Term and Definition	Example
sight words, **high-frequency words**, **irregular words** *(cont.)*	Students practice reading the sentence together. She also shows them sentences in books they have read with the word *they* in them. Then Mrs. Zamora has students collaborate with their elbow partners to come up with sentences that use the word *they*. As students share, she writes the sentences where students can see them: "They are my friends." "They are going to the baseball game." "They know how to read." She will repeat this process throughout the week with the words *was* and *you*. Students will recognize the initial and final sound in *was* and the initial sound in *you*. It is the vowel sounds that are irregular in these words. The class will practice reading poems, big books, and other texts throughout the week and point out these words so that by the end of the week, the words *they*, *was*, and *you* will be **sight words** that students will automatically be able to read when they encounter them in the future.

Word Lists

The following two lists were created using the English language words that occurred most often at that time.

Term and Definition	Example
Dolch Word List—a list of 220 high-frequency words created by Edward William Dolch in 1936. The list is arranged based on the frequency of use in reading material for students in kindergarten through second grade and does not contain any nouns. A separate list of 95 high-frequency nouns was later created.	Fisher Elementary School uses the Dolch Word List to support students as they engage with text. Ms. Battle uses strategies such as orthographic mapping to help students when they encounter these words. She teaches students to find parts of the words they know and to make connections to letter sounds they know.
Fry's Instant Word List—a list of 1,000 high-frequency words compiled by Edward Fry in 1957 and updated in 1980. This list contains all parts of speech, and the words are arranged in order of frequency of occurrence in reading material with about 100 words per grade level.	At Oak Park elementary, the teachers made the decision to use the Fry's Instant Word List across the grade levels from kindergarten to fifth grade so that each teacher would have access to a variety of high-frequency words to choose from at their grade level and it would be consistent for students. Caleb, a first grader, learned 20 high-frequency words from the Fry's Instant Word List in kindergarten. His goal is to learn 100 words by the end of first grade. Every week, his teacher teaches five words from the list, and Caleb makes connections to the parts of the words he already knows and begins looking for those words in the books he is reading. He also practices writing them. The more Caleb reads and writes these words, the sooner they will become sight words for him that he can quickly recognize.

Additional Key Term

Term and Definition	Example
orthographic mapping—a process used to store words in long-term memory; a cognitive task where readers make connections between phonemes (sounds) and graphemes (letters) to combine and recall the pronunciation, meaning, and spelling of words quickly and effortlessly	RaeAnn's favorite part of reading station time is when she gets to practice orthographic mapping on the computer. Each week, her teacher creates a Jamboard slide with the word families that they have been working on together in class. This week, they are working on *ing*. On one half of the Jamboard slide, there are 10 colored squares with *ing* typed in them. On the other half are squares with consonants, blends, and digraphs typed on them. RaeAnn's instructions are to use the computer mouse to move the squares together to form 10 words that end in *ing*. She makes these words: *ring, king, sing, thing, bring, sling, cling, string, bling,* and *sting.*

Sound-Letter Maps

Grades: K–1

Description

Making Sound-Letter Maps is a hands-on, concrete process where students map the number of sounds (phonemes) to the letters (graphemes) that represent each sound. This process facilitates orthographic mapping and the storage of words for quick and effortless retrieval during reading. Elkonin boxes are one tool used to practice sound-letter mapping.

Rationale

The purpose of using Sound-Letter Maps for orthographic mapping is so the sequence of letters in a word becomes familiar, therefore making it a sight word. Mapping the graphemes (letters) to the phonemes (sounds) helps students connect the unfamiliar to the familiar, solidifying the process of storing a word in memory. Storing words for immediate retrieval using the auditory sense (hearing the sounds) and the visual sense (seeing the letters) builds understanding of the alphabetic principle and the letters that represent sounds and is important for students becoming more proficient readers and writers.

Process

1. Provide each student with a Sound-Letter Map (see example below). There should be one box per sound provided. An example is *can*. *Can* has three sounds, /k/ /ă/ /n/, so there should be three boxes.

2. Say the word aloud.

3. Identify the sounds heard in the given word.

4. Model how to place one token per sound in each box. Tokens can be chips, cubes, cotton puffs, or other manipulatives that fit in the box and can be easily moved. In the word *can*, students would move the token into the first box when they hear /k/, another token in the second box for /ă/, and the third token in the last box for /n/.

5. Ask each student what sound they hear as they move each token.

6. Have students replace each token by writing the grapheme to represent each sound in the corresponding box.

7. Next, have students write the word outside of the boxes.

Note: For blends, the process is the same. For digraphs and trigraphs, since the letters represent one sound, there will still only be one box. When writing the letters in the box, a dotted line can be drawn to separate them if the teacher feels it will help. For example, in the word *sheet*, there are only three boxes used because only three sounds are heard (/sh/ /ē/ /t/).

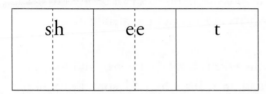

For a silent *e* at the end of the word, a diagonal line can be drawn through the box as a visual reminder of the CVE pattern.

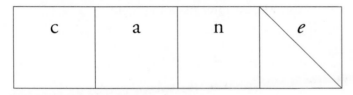

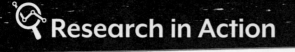

Differentiation

- Orthographic mapping and Sound-Letter Maps can be taught and practiced individually, in pairs, or in small groups.

- The number of boxes and mapping done will depend on students' letter-sound relationship proficiency.

- Pictures can be used in place of the teacher saying the word so that students can work on this skill on their own.

- Students can be given more boxes than sounds in the word, requiring that they identify the number of sounds on their own first.

- Computer applications such as Google slides or Jamboard can be used to map the sounds first as a whole class, and then students can independently type the matching letters in the boxes.

- As students become more proficient, the tokens can be removed, and sounds just shared orally. Students can also hold up a finger for each sound they hear.

- Have students use the words in sentences both orally and then in written form to practice.

- Have students look for the words in books after mapping them.

Heart Words

Grades: 2–3

Description

Heart Words is a strategy that teaches students how to read and spell irregular sight words that are largely undecodable. The irregular letter-sound relationships must be remembered "by heart" (Farrell, Hunter, and Osenga 2019; Fessel and Kennedy 2019; Really Great Reading, n.d.-a). Heart Words are considered high-frequency words that need to be read and spelled automatically. Examples of Heart Words are *have*, *some*, and *should*.

Rationale

The purpose of this strategy is to identify the parts of words that are irregular so students can learn those parts quickly as they encounter them in text. The goal is for these words to become sight words that can be read automatically.

Process

1. Display the Heart Word that will be taught. For example, *said*. Ask students which of the letter sounds they know and can decode. In *said*, it would be the initial /s/ and the final /d/.

2. Mark the irregular part of the word with a heart. In the word *said*, the *a* and *i* would be marked with hearts because the vowels do not follow a regular pattern and cannot be decoded. They must be learned "by heart."

3. Have students say the word, trace the word, and write the word.

Differentiation

-   Heart Words will change as students learn more phonics patterns and letter-sound relationships.

-   Heart Words can also be grouped by patterns to scaffold instruction.

-   Sound-Letter Maps and Elkonin boxes can be used for Heart Word lessons and practice. Students place hearts in the boxes as they map the sounds and then replace them with letters.

Moving Forward: Top Must-Dos

Understanding the differences between sight words, high-frequency words, and irregular words is important when developing lessons that will support students as they become more advanced and fluent readers. Sight-word instruction should be carefully planned, purposeful, and engaging. It should be implemented in daily whole-group lessons as well as delivered in small groups or individually to meet student needs.

Recognize the Phonics inside Sight Words

Sight words can be explicitly taught with some of the same strategies that we learned in Chapters 1 and 2 on phonological awareness and phonics. Asking students what they can identify that they know already about a sight word helps them begin to make connections. Most sight words have an initial or final sound-letter correspondence that students will recognize. Once those are pointed out, students begin to see that most sight words are decodable and can be committed to memory through the practice of reading them and writing them within the context of their books.

Help Students Recognize the Parts That Are Tricky

Examining the structure of a sight word and figuring out its parts quickly help students make connections between the known parts and the unknown. When a word is always irregular or has irregular, not easily decodable parts, the use of a strategy such as Heart Words on page 107 will help students recognize and read it more quickly.

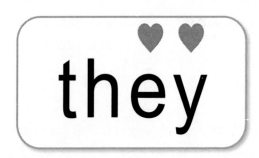

Use Orthographic Mapping

Orthographic mapping can help students match graphemes to phonemes and enable them to commit words to their long-term memory. Phoneme-grapheme mapping of sight words can be useful for beginning readers because many words on the high-frequency word lists are decodable. As students develop a proficient understanding of the alphabetic principle, they will be able to read more words, and phoneme-grapheme mapping can help students build those connections. These connections in turn allow the readers to devote their time and brain power to making meaning of text and becoming more skilled readers.

Further Considerations

Move beyond Traditional Drill Activities

Rote memorization can lead to struggles for readers who have trouble remembering more information each year. Flash cards and repetitive rewriting of words can also lead to disengagement for students who have already been able to decode the words that they are supposed to be memorizing. Using hands-on manipulatives and concrete, engaging ways to interact with sight words and practice them through orthographic mapping strategies is more beneficial for readers as they increase in automaticity.

My Teaching Checklist

Are you ready to develop students' skills with sight words so they may be strategic readers? Use this checklist to help you get started!

Sight Recognition: Familiar Words

Look Fors	Description
Students recognize sight words as multi-faceted.	• Teach students there are parts of these words that can be identified using phonics skills. • Reinforce that some parts of words will not follow traditional phonics patterns.
Students have consistent access to instruction in learning to read sight words.	• Schedule time each day for students to explicitly learn and practice high-frequency words and irregular words. • Make connections between the letter-sound relationships in high-frequency and irregular words. • Remember that even the most irregular words contain phonics patterns that students can connect to. • Teach students that there are some word parts they will need to know "by heart." • Encourage orthographic mapping of sight words through engaging, hands-on, sound-letter mapping. • Provide small-group instruction for students who are struggling with making connections between words and seeing the patterns in the high-frequency and irregular words being taught.

Chapter Summary

High-frequency words and irregular words often are decodable or have decodable parts within them. The brain is a natural pattern detector equipped to find the parts of words that are decodable, even within irregular words. This is what teachers must remember as they provide instruction. With planned, explicit, and systematic instruction in letter-sound relationships, such words can be transferred to long-term memory and become sight words.

Reflection Questions

1. What "Aha!" moments or new learning did you have about the definition of sight words and how they are taught?

2. How do you currently teach sight words?

3. In what ways does this chapter support the instruction you already provide?

4. What new learning have you gained about sight-word instruction? What new strategies for teaching sight words will you try?

Chapter 5

Fluency

From the Classroom

Nearly every week, the students engaged in reader's theater. This deliberate opportunity to engage with interesting and fun text allowed students in the second-grade classroom to reread text, practice prosody, and develop as readers. Eventually, the students grew anxious to take their weekly performances to a larger audience. They had performed for their peers in the classrooms nearby, but they desired more. It was on a Thursday morning, when students had been let into the classroom early due to rain, that two students presented their teacher with a petition. This petition asked for a parent night to show off their hard work with reader's theater.

What teacher could say no? Soon, the class was deep into the planning of an evening of grand reader's theater performances, where students could show off their fluency skills. The classroom was packed with parents, guardians, siblings, a handful of grandparents, and other family and friends as an authentic audience. Students shone. They performed five scripts that evening, having chosen those they were most excited about. Students showed their loved ones what makes for a great reader's theater performance, creating rubric handouts for their parents so they were able to connect the performances to what they had learned about reading fluency (see the rubric below).

Reader's Theater Rubric			
	Excellent	Good	Needs Improvement
pace			
expression (prosody)			
errors			
volume			
presentation			

Background Information and Research

People ask all the time, "How do kids get better at reading?" A quick answer is to read, read, read, read, read! The same holds true for increasing fluency. Fluent readers read words accurately and effortlessly. Stanislas Dehaene (2020) discusses the Science of Reading and the knowledge that reading takes mental effort. Students begin at an early age learning sounds and phonological awareness. Next, they must connect those sounds to letters (letter-sound relationships) and begin decoding through phonics instruction. Until automaticity develops through systematic and explicit teaching and practice of reading skills and strategies, and fluency increases through more opportunities to read a variety of text with accuracy and expression, students will struggle with integrating all the components of reading that make the ultimate goal of comprehension possible (Dehaene 2020; Rasinski et al. 2020).

Connection to the Rope

In the Reading Rope model (2001), Hollis Scarborough shows that skilled reading is comprised of fluent execution, coordination of word recognition, and text comprehension. Fluency is not a strand that stands alone in the Reading Rope but is the culmination of the Word Recognition strand. It includes the components of phonological awareness, decoding, and sight recognition of familiar words. Researchers agree that the components of fluency include speed, accuracy, expression, and comprehension (Kilpatrick 2019; National Reading Panel 2000b; Rasinski 2003; Rasinski et al. 2020; Shanahan 2017).

Implications for Teaching and Learning

A question many teachers ask is, "How do you increase fluency?" According to fluency expert Timothy Rasinski, oral reading practice leads to more fluent readers. Rasinski (2003) describes these four main steps for readers to practice fluency in the classroom and at home:

- **assisted reading**—students follow along as they hear text read aloud
- **practicing oral reading**—a teacher, adult, or peer provides cues when a word is read incorrectly, or the reader has trouble with decoding
- **answering questions**—students answer questions at the end of the oral reading to check comprehension and understanding
- **rereading**—students read multiple times until a text is fluently read

The next question is, "How do I provide fluency practice in addition to daily explicit phonics instruction?" Researchers agree that practice in decoding and word recognition must be continued; fluent, expressive oral reading must be modeled; and practice of authentic texts through repeated readings and activities such as reader's theater must occur, along with assisted reading practice that is scaffolded by the teacher or peers (Kilpatrick 2019; National Reading Panel 2000b; Rasinski 2003; Rasinski et al. 2020; Shanahan 2017). Teachers must be aware of text difficulty as they plan fluency instruction. They must also focus on instruction in phrasing and adding expression. Fluency practice and explicit instruction in word recognition and phonics must be planned in conjunction as complementary elements of daily reading instruction.

If readers are going to advance beyond decoding word-by-word and become fluent readers who understand reading rate, phrasing, and reading with expression, they must have daily opportunities to practice oral reading.

> If readers are going to advance beyond decoding word-by-word and become fluent readers who understand reading rate, phrasing, and reading with expression, they must have daily opportunities to practice oral reading.

Keeping Fluency Instruction and Practice Authentic

Fluency practice should be authentic and clearly tied to curriculum, rather than an inorganic add-on. Rasinski (2012) identifies performances as one way to provide students with this practice. A performance gives students real goals for practicing fluency. Through repeated reading, students will develop oral reading skills and an enhanced voice that audiences are able to connect with. Students engage in reader's theater because they each are responsible for portions of a script that they must practice for a performance. Students can also practice fluency by preparing to perform poetry. Poems should be selected to align to specific skills students are working on, to enhance content learning, or to open the doors to students' interests or passions. The wide scope of poetry available allows students to engage with poems week after week to practice fluency.

Key Terms for Teacher Understanding

The following chart provides definitions of essential terms educators need to know and an example of each one.

Term and Definition	Example
accuracy—the ability to read without making mistakes	Ms. Garcia notices that Wilisha is having trouble reading with accuracy because she is going too fast and trying to increase her speed. Wilisha is not recognizing when she misreads a word or skips it, so she is missing out on the meaning of the text. Ms. Garcia decides to help Wilisha recognize when she makes mistakes during reading with a method that requires her to pay more attention to the text.
	During small-group reading instruction, Ms. Garcia sits across from Wilisha and lets her choose a text to read out loud. Ms. Garcia tells Wilisha that if she hears her read a word inaccurately, make a mistake, or skip a word, she will tap the table as a signal for Wilisha to slow down and reread the word she just read again. This table tap will be an accuracy check for Wilisha as she reads.
	Wilisha begins to read: *The little green frog was hopping across the pool* (Ms. Garcia taps the table.) Wilisha starts again: *The little green frog was hopping across the <u>pond</u> when he saw a dart…in the sky.* (Ms. Garcia taps the table.) *when he saw a <u>dra</u>…<u>gon</u>…<u>fly</u> in the sky.* Wilisha continues to read. She rereads for accuracy when Ms. Garcia taps the table until she comes to the end of the book.
	Ms. Garcia asks Wilisha how the table tap helped her. Wilisha says that it made her slow down and pay more attention to each word. Ms. Garcia checks
	(Continued)

Term and Definition	Example
accuracy *(cont.)*	Wilisha's comprehension, and she can retell the story and correctly answer a few questions about the meaning. They will continue these accuracy checks to help Wilisha work on accuracy and slow down to double-check herself while reading.
automaticity—the quick, effortless, and accurate recognition (or decoding) of words in reading	Pauline, a second grader, has been struggling with automaticity, so her teacher decides to help her make a flip book to practice onset and rime with word families they have recently learned in class. The first flip book is for the *ill* rime, or word family. Pauline folds a piece of paper in half horizontally. On one half of the paper, she writes the rime *ill*. Her teacher gives her index cards, and together they write onsets that will create new words when paired with *ill*. They start with the consonants: *b, d, f, g, h, j, k, m, p, s, t,* and *w*. Then they write blends: *fr, kr, tr, dr, sk, st, gr,* and *sp*. Then, they write digraphs and trigraphs: *ch, shr,* and *thr*. The teacher punches holes in the index cards and keeps them on rings. Pauline practices her automaticity with more than 20 words she can make with her new onset-rime flip book.

(Continued)

Term and Definition	Example
expression—making your words and speech lively; appropriate fluctuations in pitch, timing, emphasis, and intonation when reading aloud; expression can convey the understanding of meaning	Mr. Michaels notices that his second-grade students sound like robots when they are reading out loud. He decides to work on improving his students' expression in a new way. To start their reading time together, he gives them directions to come to the carpet using a robotic voice—choppy and monotone. They laugh and ask him why he is talking that way. He tells them that just as our talking voices should be smooth and have expression, so should our reading-out-loud voices. He goes on to say that when we read, we need to practice making our voice lively by getting louder and softer and going slower or faster. "We don't want to sound like a robot when we read," he says.

He reads a sentence and has them echo read after him, mimicking his speed, phrasing, tone, and expression. The first sentence he writes on the board is: "I am not a robot!" He reads it like a robot first and has the students repeat it sounding like robots. They think that is funny and like trying it out. He knows it will help them get the robot voices out of their systems. He next reads the same sentence with expression, emphasizing the word *not* and making his voice louder. He then has them repeat the sentence with expression. They practice a few more sentences that way.

Mr. Michaels then has students practice some sentences in silly voices, such as sounding like a teeny tiny mouse, or a mean monster, or a baby. He can now remind them about not reading with a robot voice if he needs to encourage them to use expression when reading out loud. They also can give characters different expressive voices, like the ones they have practiced. |

Term and Definition	Example
fluency—the ability to read with speed, accuracy, and expression	Tonya, Dee, Diego, Matt, and Allison are ready to perform their reader's theater script for Ms. Tiet and the rest of their second-grade class. Their performance is based on *The Three Little Pigs*. They have been rereading their script and practicing their lines every day so they will be able to read with fluency. Tonya is the narrator. She had to work the most on her accuracy because the narrator's part had some words she had never seen before. She used her knowledge of phonics to help her, and then she repeatedly read her part at home so she would not make any mistakes. Dee, Allison, and Matt are the three pigs. They practiced reading their parts with expression all week because there are a lot of exclamation points and squealing sounds in their lines. Diego is the Big Bad Wolf, so he deepened his voice as he read. He also worked on phrasing, and he made sure he did not read too fast. When the group stands in front of the class to perform their reader's theater script, they are all reading fluently using proper speed, accuracy, and expression. Ms. Tiet and the other students love the performance and clap wildly after the students are done.

(Continued)

Term and Definition	Example
phrasing—grouping words together when reading to sound more like talking instead of reading one word at a time	Zoe likes to point to each word as she reads, but it has caused her to read word-for-word and slowed down her reading rate. Her teacher wants her to become more fluent. She helps her practice phrasing using prepositional phrases and phrases that contain sight words, which she will be able to decode easily. Ms. Campos knows that Zoe still likes to touch the words, so she teaches her to "scoop the phrases" by putting her finger on the preposition, or first word of the phrase, and scooping her finger under the other words as she reads them until she touches the final word. When she scoops, she cannot lift her finger to touch each word; she must smoothly scoop, or slide, her finger under the entire phrase. These are examples of phrases Zoe practices scooping: *by the doghouse, on the floor, around the bed, in the tree,* and *down the slide.* After Zoe practices scooping phrases out of context, Ms. Campos writes sentences using these phrases and others for Zoe to practice: *The dog is by the doghouse. She is running around the bed. The kids like to slide down the slide.* Ms. Campos helps Zoe transition from using her finger to using a marker to scoop phrases as she reads. Eventually Zoe will extend the scooping practice to additional phrases and sections of text to help her as she reads longer texts.

Term and Definition	Example
prosody—reading with expression	Genesis wants to read a poem during the announcements for the first day of fall. He knows all the words and can read them quickly, but he gets nervous and starts to read slowly and in a monotone voice. Genesis asks his teacher how he can improve his reading. His teacher tells him he needs to practice reading with expression, or *prosody*. His teacher models reading the poem first. She makes sure to emphasize the words that are characteristics of fall by making her voice change pitch and volume. For example, in the line that says, "…the leaves are falling, falling, falling from way up high in the trees," she models lowering her voice every time she repeats the word *falling*. She also gets louder and makes her voice higher-pitched when she reads the words *way up high in the trees*. She teaches Genesis that the commas between the words *falling, falling, falling* tell the reader to pause, so she rereads those words showing him what that sounds like. They also look at the meaning of certain words in the poem. The author uses the word *crunch* when he describes the leaves under your feet. Genesis's teacher tells him that *crunch* is an onomatopoeia, or sound word, so he can make a crunch sound as he reads the word. After she reads the entire poem modeling prosody for him, she reads the poem again, having him repeat each line with prosody. They go line by line practicing reading with expression. Next, she has him read the poem with prosody by himself. Genesis promises to practice reading the poem with prosody every day until it is his turn to read it during the announcements.

(Continued)

Term and Definition	Example
speed (reading rate)— the rate at which a person reads printed text; usually calculated by the number of words read per minute	Mr. Kessner provides opportunities for his students to practice fluent reading. One of the measures they use to evaluate their fluency is speed. After a one-minute fluency practice, students count the words they read correctly. Using a fluency rubric, they assess their reading rate.

Repeated Reading

Grades: K–1

Description

Students orally read a short piece of text more than one time, usually a minimum of three times.

Rationale

Repeated reading improves reading, helping readers gain automaticity by not having to focus attention on decoding words the entire time (Shanahan 2017). Oral repeated readings allow students to use additional sensory cues as they view text, listen carefully, and read out loud with expression and purpose (Rasinski 2003). The purpose of repeated reading is to increase oral reading fluency, word recognition, and comprehension.

Process

1. Choose a short piece of text for students to read orally. This text should contain words that are high utility and will transfer to multiple other texts. Repeated exposure to sight words and easily decodable vocabulary will transfer to more than just this one text and increase students' fluency more quickly. Choose texts that are not too easy so that students get more practice with building automaticity and fluency strategies.

2. Model reading aloud for students. Have students read independently or with partners as you bring a small group or individual students together to read aloud. Listen to individual students read and check for accuracy as they read the first time, correcting any mistakes.

3. Have students read the text orally again, this time concentrating on reading rate and phrasing.

4. When students do a repeated reading for the third time, have them read with expression.

5. At the end, ask students at least one comprehension question, or have them complete a comprehension task to connect fluency and making meaning.

6. Have students continue to read to partners as you call another small group together.

Differentiation

- Pair students to practice repeated reading while you circulate around the room to listen to them read out loud to each other.

- Students can use poems or familiar text to practice repeated reading during independent reading time or at reading stations.

- Teachers can have poems or short text placed around the room for students to repeatedly read.

- Recite poems together as a whole class during carpet time, then have those texts available for students during independent reading.

Modeled Reading

Grades: 2–3

Description

Teachers orally read to students and draw attention to the natural way their voices sound when pronouncing words accurately and reading with expression. Modeled Reading is also known as Echo Reading because after teachers model how a text should sound, students read aloud, echoing what they just heard.

Rationale

Modeled Reading develops fluency by demonstrating to students the importance of accurate reading and appropriate expression when reading aloud.

Process

1. Model reading a short piece of text in a slow, choppy, unexpressive way. Ask students how it sounded to hear the text that way. Let them share their impressions.

2. Model reading the same passage again in a fluent way—flowing smoothly and reading with expression. Ask students which they preferred as they listened to the text—the slow and unexpressive reading, or the fluent reading.

3. Reread the text again, having students echo read after you. Students should echo the words as well as the expression that is modeled. This can be done line by line at first, eventually moving to multiple lines, and then using the entire text, depending on length.

Differentiation

- Model fluent reading by sharing a text on a large screen, written out on chart paper large enough for everyone to see, or by reading a big book.

- Choose different voices and expressions for the characters, and have students imitate when you model reading.

- Students can echo read with partners by taking turns reading lines in a poem or short text.

Assisted Reading

Grades: 4–5

Description

Assisted Reading involves activities such as choral reading, paired reading, and using recordings of readings. These activities support students' fluency beyond the modeling provided by the teacher.

Rationale

Assisted Reading allows students to both hear a text read fluently and read the text at the same time. This has been shown to increase fluency as well as comprehension (Rasinski 2003).

Process

Choral Reading

Have students read different types of text together, such as the school motto, a class saying, or a daily poem or song. The teacher or a student can assign students numbers and give each group a specific place to join in, or students can begin when they hear an agreed-upon signal.

Paired Reading

Pair students together. Have each pair practice reading a piece of text at the same time out loud. Each student will hear their partner read as they are also reading and can correct any inaccuracies or mimic what they hear in a risk-free environment.

Recorded Readings

Use audiobooks or read-along ebooks that students can listen to as a whole class or with headphones at stations. Have students follow along with the text as they hear it read fluently. Ask students to stop every few minutes and tell you or tell a partner what they heard or what the text is about. Another method is to have students read along with the closed captions when watching videos or TV shows.

Differentiation

In Assisted Reading, the words in the text are meant to be read out loud together. Both readers set the pace together if it is two students at the same level. If the readers are an adult and a child, the adult reads at the pace of the child to model good fluency for them.

- After reading together, pairs can also take turns reading out loud to each other to work on their fluency.

- Students can record themselves reading out loud with computer applications, such as VoiceThread. They can then listen to themselves to check their fluency and read along with themselves to practice. Students can also record themselves a second time to see their improvement.

Reader's Theater

Secondary Grades

Description

Reader's theater combines reading practice with performance. Students perform by reading aloud portions of a script. Typically, reader's theater is focused on reading, not on using costumes or props (which can distract from the practice of reading).

Rationale

Reader's theater provides students with authentic purpose for rereading text. Since repeated reading supports students' increasing automaticity, this process helps students better understand what is read while engaging in purposeful rereading.

Process

1. Choose a script. Begin with short, easy scripts to ensure students understand the procedure of reader's theater.

2. Have students work in small groups. First, group all students together by the parts they will read. This way, they get to practice all the same lines as their groups. Then have them jigsaw into groups where every student plays a different part.

3. Establish a practice schedule for students. This schedule can become a routine that students engage with regularly. Below, find suggestions for a weekly plan (Rasinski 2012).

    Monday

    - Display the script for all to see.
    - Read the script aloud with the whole class.
    - Ensure all students comprehend the text.
    - Allow students to read portions of the script chorally or using echo reading.

Tuesday–Thursday

- Provide time for students to practice their parts.
- Rehearse homogeneously so students can practice with peers who are reading the same part.
- Rehearse heterogeneously to create the entire performance experience.

Friday

- Provide an opportunity for students to perform their reader's theater scripts in front of an audience.

Act 2	
Narrator:	The boys slowly cross the street, looking down at their feet. Jason's older brother, Chris, watches as they walk into the house. He's cramming his mouth full of chips while flipping channels with the remote control.
Chris:	"What's up?"
Mike:	"We have to write poems for Kindness Week. Poems are yucky."
Jason:	"Yeah, they're about flowers and kittens!"
Chris:	"They are not!"
Jason:	"They are so!"
Chris:	"Poems can be fun, smart, silly, and funny."

Differentiation

- Allow students to work together to perform a part.
- Allow students to record themselves reading for performance.
- Provide students with a range of parts that best support their needs for reading practice.
- Provide small-group instruction to preteach content or vocabulary to support students' reading of the reader's theater text.

Moving Forward: Top Must-Dos

Fluency lessons and activities should be carefully planned, purposeful, and engaging. They should be implemented in daily whole-group lessons as well as delivered in small groups or individually to meet student needs. Preparing to perform for an audience provides students with opportunities to practice fluency and is important for ensuring they become more proficient and fluent readers.

Provide Ample Opportunities to Practice Reading

To become more proficient readers, students must practice fluent reading. When first encountering new text, students' reading will be stilted, and they will focus all their energy on decoding words that they do not already have in their sight word vocabularies. Once they become more skilled at decoding, their reading rates and accuracy will improve. Next, students will gain fluency as they practice phrasing and prosody. With more opportunities to read aloud, they will begin to effortlessly put all these components together. This will lead to more confident readers who comprehend text, who increase their sight word banks and their vocabularies, and who ultimately enjoy reading.

Allow Students to Encounter Words Over and Over

As students engage with multiple texts daily for repeated reading, modeled reading, and assisted reading, they will be exposed to more known and unknown words. Repeated reading, especially, will help students become more efficient at decoding new words. With more practice, those unfamiliar words will become familiar. As more words are encountered and students become more proficient decoders, they will gain automaticity.

Build Understanding That Fluent Reading Equals Greater Comprehension

Giving students a text that is far above their reading level and asking them to read it out loud and to comprehend what it means is a good way to initially help them see that fluency (accuracy, rate, and prosody) and comprehension are dependent upon each other. Even if they can decode the words, the time and brain power required to read word by word will likely cause students to miss the overall meaning. Begin fluency instruction with high-interest texts, such as poems, songs, nursery rhymes, or chants. Then use extended pieces of text such as reader's theater scripts that connect to holidays, unit themes, or science and social studies content to provide engaging fluency practice.

Further Considerations

Fluency Is Not Equal to Speed Alone

When students focus only on speed and word accuracy, they are concentrating on quickly decoding words and often miss the meaning of the words. And, by thinking only of how fast they are reading, students may read in monotone voices without expression and phrasing. Speed (or reading rate), accuracy, and prosody working together lead to greater comprehension of text.

Work on Fluency beyond the Primary Grades

As texts get harder and words get longer in upper grades, the struggle with fluency can become greater. Keith Stanovich (1986) used the idea of "the Matthew Effect" (or as the saying goes, "The rich get richer and the poor get poorer") to describe older readers with low word-recognition strategies. It leads to a greater gap in fluency skills, which in turn causes a loss of interest in reading overall. The older students get while struggling with fluency, the less time they will spend reading when given the opportunity, leading to even greater reading deficits. Teachers must continue to engage students in reading strategies that build fluency as they move beyond foundational reading skills and into longer and more complex varieties of text.

My Teaching Checklist

Are you ready to develop students' fluency skills so they may be strategic readers? Use this checklist to help you get started!

Fluency	
Look Fors	**Description**
Students have consistent access to explicit fluency instruction.	• Schedule time each day to explicitly teach fluency. • Provide small-group instruction for students who are struggling with fluency.
Students have frequent and varied opportunities to practice fluency.	• Have students practice fluency with a variety of texts and media, including books, graphics, and other technology sources. • Include active engagement strategies to help students practice fluency, such as repeated readings, modeled readings, and assisted readings. • Provide students with a variety of texts and multimedia to practice fluency. • Plan times for students to perform for audiences.

Chapter Summary

Much research has been done over the years on fluency and oral reading (Rasinski 2003; Rasinski et al. 2020; National Reading Panel 2000b). Oral reading practice increases word recognition, fluency, and comprehension. Repeated reading, modeled reading, and assisted reading lead to improvement of reading skills and greater reading achievement. When students can decode words quickly and effortlessly, develop automaticity, and read at an increased rate while using expression and correct phrasing, they are able to focus on making meaning. This blending of word recognition, fluency, and comprehension is what leads to strategic and skilled readers.

Reflection Questions

1. How do you include fluency practice during the day?

2. What teacher and student resources do you have for fluency instruction?

3. What new learning have you gained about fluency instruction? What new strategies will you try?

Chapter 6

Seize Every Moment to Create Lifelong Readers

by Alan Becker
Greenville, North Carolina

Recognizing that word-recognition instruction should not be restricted to the language arts block is essential to ensuring that students are able to use their word recognition skills across content and contexts. There are no boundaries defining when reading instruction begins and ends. In fact, the erroneous belief that reading instruction only happens within the language arts block can be a contributor to low student performance. Let's examine a powerful story of a teacher who decided that word recognition was going to be a part of every lesson in the school day, continuously and intentionally building and reinforcing skills.

Discovering the Power of Cross-Content Connections

Ms. Martinez decided that if all of her fourth-grade students were going to be successful with word recognition, instruction and reinforcement in all the content areas would benefit them. She knew that her students had a foundational understanding of letter sounds, blends, and digraphs, and she decided that a continued focus on word parts would support her students even further. Using the scope and sequence, she chose root words and affixes as the specific area of focus. In the text she was using to teach the new reading standard, she noticed many negative prefixes. She decided that the spelling and vocabulary instruction would include these prefixes: *dis–*, *im–*, *in–*, *mis–*, *non–*, and *un–*. From the text, she chose these vocabulary words: *dishonest, inexpensive, unprepared, illegal, nonsense,* and *immoral*. She developed the word work/vocabulary list for the week with these words, but she also added a few more words with negative prefixes: *impolite, incorrect, nonfiction,* and *unusual*. She chose to introduce students to the meanings of the prefixes through direct instruction and modeling on Monday and then spent 15 minutes each following day on word-work activities.

After the word-work activities, she supported students as they engaged with rigorous text, teaching her comprehension standard. When they came across one of the vocabulary words, the class used the skills they had practiced, focusing on the root word and its meaning, while Ms. Martinez modeled how to also use context to determine the meaning of roots. At the end of the week, students were given a quick assessment to determine the effectiveness of the instruction for that lesson. Ms. Martinez really wanted to be sure that her students grasped and retained the meanings of the negative prefixes, so she made certain she infused additional connections while planning for other subjects.

> Repetition and practice supporting word recognition are integral. Remember, opportunities to practice word recognition skills in the content areas are abundant, and students skills' improve with increased exposure.

Beginning with mathematics, Ms. Martinez planned to teach interpreting a divisor and quotient in a division equation by representing the number of equal groups and the number of objects in each group. In the past, she had always used the language "not equal" in her modeling and knew that she could now use "unequal" instead. This gave her the opportunity to very quickly review that the meaning of *equal* when combined with the prefix *un–* means "not equal." At this point in the planning process, she decided to add *unequal* as one of her mathematic vocabulary words to use and display for students.

She took the same methodical approach with her science instruction, ensuring that students would have opportunities to practice their word recognition skills in science content as well. She was preparing to teach a unit on forces and motion, and this afforded her the perfect opportunity to integrate the word *unbalanced* when she was modeling how to determine which forces are unbalanced. As this became routine, a dive into social studies units provided additional opportunities for word-recognition instruction and practice. Students would soon be engaged in learning about citizenship in the United States. As she glanced through the texts about citizenship, she noticed the word *noncitizen* and quickly wrote it down in her planner to make sure she highlighted it for students. It was clear that a seamless integration of these word-recognition skills across her core content areas was possible. She turned her attention to devising a plan to reinforce the meanings during instruction.

Ms. Martinez created a Focus Board at the front of her room (see figure 6.1 below). At the top of the board, she listed these prefixes: *dis–*, *im–*, *in–*, *mis–*, *non–*, and *un–* and included a placeholder for the definition, "not." Below the prefixes and definition, she drew two columns. In one column she wrote the academic vocabulary words she chose, and in the other column she wrote only the root words that were used. At the bottom of the Focus Board, she drew a box and labeled it, "Examples We Have Found," where she could list examples of words that students found during independent reading, using the highlighted prefixes for the lesson. Her plan was to give students visual access to the Focus Board during her instruction in the different subjects and use it to model the meaning of the words during her lessons. Another thing that Ms. Martinez did with the Focus Board was to tell students to use the vocabulary words and the root words when writing independently or as part of an instructional activity. For this, she knew she had to make the request quantitative, so she challenged students to use two to three words from the board.

Figure 6.1—Focus Board

Prefixes: *dis–*, *im–*, *in–*, *mis–*, *non–*, *un–* Definition: "not"	
Vocabulary Words	**Root Words**
dishonest	honest
unprepared	prepare
inexpensive	expense
illegal	legal
nonsense	sense
immoral	moral
impolite	polite
incorrect	correct
unusual	usual
nonfiction	fiction
unequal	equal
noncitizen	citizen
unbalanced	balance
Examples We Have Found:	

As Ms. Martinez continued the week's lessons in reading, mathematics, science, and social studies, she made sure to use the words she chose and modeled how to use them correctly each time, reinforcing the meanings of the words using the prefix definitions. At the end of the week, she administered a word work/vocabulary assessment, hiding the words written around the room. Rather than have students match the definitions with the words used throughout the week, she chose different words that included the negative prefixes taught all week and placed them in sentences and paragraphs. Students were assessed on how accurately they could determine the definition of the new words while also using the available surrounding context provided by the sentence. Her goal was to provide her students with an assessment that was an extension of the lesson and that continued the learning process as well as allowing students to showcase deepened comprehension skills when recognizing the words. At the end of the week, she noticed that her students performed much better on the assessments and were using the words more often in their writing weeks later.

> For the average student, words and their parts need to be repeated 10–15 times with a wide range of variation for students to internalize them and make use of them correctly. (Lemoine, Levy, and Hutchinson 1993).

As we share this story about Ms. Martinez, the best practices in word recognition unfold in front of us. For the average student, words and their parts need to be repeated 10–15 times with a wide range of variation for students to internalize them and make use of them correctly. Students who are struggling readers may need to have more exposure to words, and students who are above grade-level in reading may need less (Lemoine, Levy, and Hutchinson 1993). Although this story is an example of more advanced word identification strategies, the same protocol can be used in the primary grades where the focus is alphabetic knowledge, phonics, and phonemic awareness.

When we walk through the doors of a kindergarten or first grade classroom, we should observe students engaged as the teacher uses a big book to model letter sounds and phonetic principles. As students listen to the text, they can engage with a range of skills from alphabetic principle, to blending, to syllabication. Sometimes, we may even see a student using a pointer to track the sounds in a word or the words in a sentence. We may find Wikki Stix® or highlighting tape that students use to select specific sounds in science journals or underlining to identify the short vowels in a social studies article. Teachers may be leading students in singing or reciting a poem they learned earlier in their developmental stages. When finished, students often can write independently about the subject matter of the story or text and focus on using familiar words learned during carpet time. Repetition and practice supporting word recognition are integral. Remember, opportunities to practice word recognition skills in the content areas are abundant, and students skills' improve with increased exposure.

Another Look: The Science Classroom

Let's look at weaving these practices into a block of time dedicated for science instruction, more specifically, life sciences and ecosystems. I was working with a teacher who absolutely loved teaching science. It is a great part of a student's day, especially when they can explore and engage with the science topic. One of the most impactful adjustments that we made together in her classroom was the addition of high-interest science texts as part of the lesson. The great thing about the texts was that they were aligned to the state standards, the language usage was repetitive, and they afforded the opportunity to again focus on previously taught word recognition practices. Here are two sentences from one of the texts:

- "Living things need light."
- "Living things need water."

We have the opportunity with this text to review letter sounds within one-syllable words and move into using letter sounds with two-syllable words using *light* and *water*.

- In *light*, the onset sound is /l/ and the rime sound is /īt/.
- In *water*, the onset sound is /wa/ and the rime sound is /ter/.

We can also point out to students the different phonemes contained within each word as review.

- The word *light* contains three phonemes: /l/ /ī/ /t/.
- The word *water* contains four phonemes: /w/ /ä/ /t/ /er/.

All this instruction can be covered after reading aloud the scientific text with students. The teacher can model the sequence of phonemic awareness by reading each sentence that begins with a repetitive phrase, helping students segment the sentences into words, showcase the syllables in each word, break a word into its onset and rime, and lastly, segment the one- and two-syllable words into phonemes.

Another Look: The Social Studies Classroom

When students are engaged in learning about three-syllable words, this learning can be infused into an approaching social studies unit. Suppose the unit is focused on contributions made by people from different countries and how those contributions have helped shape the United States. It is easy to use a text that engages students with the subject matter of the Statue of Liberty while we read and discuss its origin and significance. As we read, we can reinforce the word recognition skills learned during the reading block, using the word *liberty*.

- "It is called the Statue of Liberty."
- "We call her Lady Liberty."

After reading each sentence, follow the sequence of phonemic awareness instruction: Review previous skills, and introduce newly discovered word-recognition skills in the context of the text. First segment the sentence into words, showcase the syllables, and then segment the three-syllable word into phonemes.

- The word *liberty* has three syllables: li/ber/ty.

After the social studies content is taught to students and the word-recognition skills are introduced or reviewed within this block of time, the opportunity is perfect to blend both areas into a student-guided activity. Have students write a poem that includes the word *liberty* and allows them to show you what they learned about the social studies content. An example of a poem is on the following page.

Mighty, Tidy, Liberty

Mighty, tidy, Liberty
Shining in the sun
Mighty, tidy, Liberty
You must weigh ten tons

Mighty, tidy, Liberty
Your flame, it burns so bright
Mighty, tidy, Liberty
Who lights that flame each night?

Mighty, tidy, Liberty
You came to us from France
Mighty, tidy, Liberty
With you I cannot dance

Mighty, tidy, Liberty
You show that we are free
Mighty, tidy, Liberty
The U.S. is the best place to be.

Chapter Summary

Reading practice is a crucial ingredient to help develop fluent word recognition, and there are many opportunities during the school day to strengthen this skill in our students. When students are engaged in content-area learning, you have their attention to practice one of the most important skills they need to be successful in school and in life. If the goal is fluent, grade-level readers in our classrooms, we must allow students to practice reading in all content areas. Now, go and seize every moment to help students learn the lifelong skill of reading.

Gregory Alan Becker Jr. provides professional development on best practices for curriculum and instruction. He specializes in the content areas of math, English language arts, and social studies and works with school districts, teachers, and educational trainers. He previously served as an elementary school teacher and a district elementary education specialist with Pitt County Schools in Greenville, North Carolina.

References

Archer, Anita L. 2011. *Explicit Instruction: Effective and Efficient Teaching.* New York: Guilford Press.

Blevins, Wiley. 2020. "A Fresh Look at Phonics: Make Instruction Active and Engaging to Turn Students into Skilled Readers." *Principal* 100 (2): 16–19. www.naesp.org/principal/november-december-2020/.

Bottari, Marjori. 2020. "Transitioning from Word Walls to Sound Walls." *Reading Rockets.* www.readingrockets.org/article/transitioning-word-walls-sound -walls#:~:text=What%20is%20a%20sound%20wall,in%20words%20are%20 co%2Darticulated.

Coan, Sharon. 2012. *Big Pig.* Huntington Beach, CA: Teacher Created Materials.

Dehaene, Stanislas. 2020. *How We Learn: Why Brains Learn Better Than Any New Machine . . . For Now.* New York: Viking.

Dugan, Christine. 2012. *Targeted Phonics: Short Vowel Rimes Teacher's Guide.* Huntington Beach, CA: Teacher Created Materials.

Duke, Nell K. 2022. "What Wordle Reminds Us About Effective Phonics and Spelling Instruction." ASCD (blog), January 28, 2022. www.ascd.org/blogs/ what-wordle-reminds-us-about-effective-phonics-and-spelling-instruction.

Duke, Nell K., and Kelly B. Cartwright. 2021. "The Science of Reading Progresses: Communicating Advances Beyond the Simple View of Reading." *Reading Research Quarterly* (Special Issue) 56 (S1): S25–S44.

Duke, Nell K., and Heidi Anne E. Mesmer. 2018. "Phonics Faux Pas: Avoiding Instructional Missteps in Teaching Letter-Sound Relationships." *American Educator* 42 (4): 12–16. www.aft.org/ae/winter2018-2019/duke_mesmer.

Ehri, Linnea C. 1995. "Phases of Development in Learning to Read Words by Sight." *Journal of Research in Reading* 18 (2): 116–125. doi.org/10.1111/j.1467-9817.1995.tb00077.x.

———. 1998. "Grapheme-Phoneme Knowledge Is Essential to Learning to Read Words in English." In *Word Recognition in Beginning Literacy*, edited by J. L. Metsala and L. C. Ehri, 3–40. Mahwah: NJ: Lawrence Erlbaum Associates.

———. 2014. "Orthographic Mapping in the Acquisition of Sight Word Reading, Spelling Memory, and Vocabulary Learning." *Scientific Studies of Reading* 18 (1): 5–21. doi.org/10.1080/10888438.2013.819356.

Ehri, Linnea C., and Sandra McCormick. 1998. "Phases of Word Learning: Implications for Instruction with Delayed and Disabled Readers." *Reading & Writing Quarterly* 14 (2), 135–163.

Ehri, Linnea C., Simone R. Nunes, Dale M. Willows, Barbara Valeska Schuster, Zohreh Yaghoub-Zadeh, and Timothy Shanahan. 2001. "Phonemic Awareness Instruction Helps Children Learn to Read: Evidence from the National Reading Panel's Meta-Analysis." *Reading Research Quarterly*, 36 (3): 250–287.

Ehri, Linnea C., and Margaret J. Snowling. 2004. "Developmental Variation in Word Recognition." In *Handbook of Language and Literacy: Development and Disorders*, edited by C. A. Stone, E. R. Silliman, B. J. Ehren, and K. Apel, 433–460. New York: Guilford.

Farrell, Linda, Michael Hunter, and Tina Osenga. 2019. "A New Model for Teaching High-Frequency Words." *Reading Rockets*. www.readingrockets.org /article/new-model-teaching-high-frequency-words/.

Fessel, Elizabeth and Pamela Kennedy. 2019. "Teaching Sight Words According to Science." *ODE Literacy Academy*. education.ohio.gov/getattachment/Topics /Learning-in-Ohio/Literacy/Striving-Readers-Comprehensive-Literacy-Grant /Literacy-Academy/2-07-Teaching-Sight-Words-According-to-Science.pdf. aspx?lang=en-US.

Foorman, B., N. Beyler, K. Borradaile, M. Coyne, C. A. Denton, J. Dimino, J. Furgeson, L. Hayes, J. Henke, L. Justice, B. Keating, W. Lewis, S. Sattar, A. Streke, R. Wagner, and S. Wissel. 2016. *Foundational Skills to Support Reading for Understanding in Kindergarten Through 3rd Grade*. NCEE 2016-4008. Washington, DC: U.S. Department of Education.

Gough, Philip B., and William E. Tunmer. 1986. "Decoding, Reading, and Reading Disability." *Remedial and Special Education* 7 (1): 6–10.

Hasbrouck, Jan. 2017. *Quick Phonics Screener*, 3rd ed. Seattle: JH Educational Services.

Jackson, Robyn and Allison Zmuda. 2014. "Four (Secret) Keys to Student Engagement." *Educational Leadership*, 72 (1), 18–24.

Kilpatrick, David A. 2015. *Essentials of Assessing, Preventing, and Overcoming Reading Difficulties*. Hoboken, NJ: Wiley.

———. 2016. *Equipped for Reading Success: A Comprehensive, Step-by-Step Program for Developing Phonemic Awareness and Fluent Word Recognition*. Syracuse, New York: Casey & Kirsch.

———. 2019. "Assessing, Preventing, and Overcoming Reading Difficulties" (online course). Colorado Department of Education. sitesed.cde.state.co.us /course/view.php?id=132#section-1.

Lemoine, Hope E., Betty A. Levy, and Ann Hutchinson. 1993. "Increasing the Naming Speed of Poor Readers: Representations Formed Across Repetitions. *Journal of Experimental Child Psychology*, 55 (3): 297–328. doi.org/10.1006 /jecp.1993.1018.

Moats, Louisa Cook. 2020a. *Speech to Print: Language Essentials for Teachers*. Baltimore: Paul H. Brookes.

———. 2020b. "Teaching Reading Is Rocket Science." *American Educator*. Summer, 2020.

Nagy, William E., and Richard C. Anderson. 1984. "How Many Words Are There in Printed School English?" *Reading Research Quarterly* 19 (3): 304–30. doi.org/10.2307/747823.

National Reading Panel (U.S.) and National Institute of Child Health and Human Development (U.S.). 2000a. *Report of the National Reading Panel: Teaching Children to Read: An Evidence-based Assessment of the Scientific Research Literature on Reading and Its Implications for Reading Instruction*. Bethesda, MD: U.S. Dept. of Health and Human Services, Public Health Service, National Institutes of Health, National Institute of Child Health and Human Development.

———. 2000b. *Report of the National Reading Panel: Teaching Children to Read (Reports of the Subgroups)*. Bethesda, MD: U.S. Dept. of Health and Human Services, Public Health Service, National Institutes of Health, National Institute of Child Health and Human Development.

Pimentel, Susan. 2018. "Why Doesn't Every Teacher Know the Research on Reading Instruction?" *Education Week*. October 26, 2018. www.edweek.org/teaching -learning/opinion-why-doesnt-every-teacher-know-the-research-on-reading -instruction/2018/10.

Rasinski, Timothy V. 2003. *The Fluent Reader: Oral Reading Strategies for Building Word Recognition, Fluency, and Comprehension*. New York: Scholastic.

———. 2012. "Why Reading Fluency Should be Hot." *The Reading Teacher*, 65 (8): 516–522.

Rasinski, Timothy and Lorraine Griffith. 2011. *Fluency Through Practice and Performance*. Huntington Beach, CA: Shell Education.

Rasinski, Timothy, Nancy Padak, Rick Newton, and Evangeline Newton. 2019. *Building Vocabulary Teacher's Guide*. Huntington Beach, CA: Teacher Created Materials.

———. 2020. *Building Vocabulary with Greek and Latin Roots*, 2nd ed. Huntington Beach, CA: Shell Education.

Really Great Reading. n.d.-a. "Heart Word Magic: Helping Students Learn to Read and Spell High Frequency Words." www.reallygreatreading.com/heart-word-magic

———. n.d.-b. "What is Scarborough's Reading Rope?" www.reallygreatreading.com/content/scarboroughs-reading-rope/.

Reutzel, D. Ray. 2015. "Early Literacy Research: Findings Primary Grade Teachers Will Want to Know." *The Reading Teacher*. 69 (1): 14–24.

Scarborough, Hollis S. 2001. "Connecting Early Language and Literacy to Later Reading (Dis)abilities: Evidence, Theory, and Practice." *In Handbook for Research in Early Literacy*, edited by S. Neuman and D. Dickinson, 97–110. New York: Guilford Press.

Seidenberg, Mark S. 2017. *Language at the Speed of Sight*. New York: Basic Books.

Shanahan, Timothy. 2017. "Everything You Wanted to Know About Repeated Reading." Reading Rockets: Shanahan on Literacy (blog), August 4, 2017. www.readingrockets.org/blogs/shanahan-literacy/everything-you-wanted-know-about-repeated-reading.

Stanovich, Keith E. 1986. "Matthew Effects in Reading: Some Consequences of Individual Differences in the Acquisition of Literacy." *Reading Research Quarterly*, 21 (4), 360–407.

Stewart, Laura. n.d. *The Science of Reading: Evidence for a New Era of Reading Instruction.* Zaner-Bloser. www.zaner-bloser.com/research/the-science -of-reading-evidence-for-a-new-era-of-reading-instruction.php/.

Wardle, Josh. 2021. *Wordle.* www.powerlanguage.co.uk/wordle/.

Willingham, Daniel. 2016. "Knowledge and Practice: The Real Keys to Critical Thinking." *Knowledge Matters Issue Brief* 1 (March). knowledgematterscampaign.org/wp-content/uploads/2016/05/Willingham-brief .pdf.

———. 2017. *The Reading Mind: A Cognitive Approach to Understanding How the Mind Reads.* San Francisco: Jossey-Bass.

Wolf, Gail M. 2016. "Letter-Sound Reading: Teaching Preschool Children Print-to -Sound Processing." *Early Childhood Education Journal*, 44 (1): 11–19. link.springer.com/article/10.1007/s10643-014-0685-y.

Yopp, Hallie Kay, and Ruth Helen Yopp. 2022. *Purposeful Play for Early Childhood Phonological Awareness*, 2nd ed. Huntington Beach, CA: Shell Education.

Glossary

accuracy—the ability to read without making mistakes

affix—any word part that attaches to the beginning or end of a word; an umbrella term for *prefixes* and *suffixes*

automaticity—the quick, effortless, and accurate recognition (or decoding) of words in reading

base—a root that carries the basic meaning of a word; a base may be a word part or a stand-alone word; some use the terms *base* and *root* interchangeably

compound words—words that are created when two or more individual words are joined together to make a new word with a new meaning; there are three types of compound words: **closed compound words** (*football, butterfly, cowboy*), **open compound words** (*living room, coffee table, ice cream*), and **hyphenated compound words** (*merry-go-round, part-time*)

consonant—any of the following 21 letters in the alphabet: *b, c, d, f, g, h, j, k, l, m, n, p, q, r, s, t, v, w, x, y, z*; these letters represent consonant sounds that are made when air is partially blocked by the tongue, teeth, or lips when making a sound while speaking

consonant clusters—when two or more consonants are next to each other in a word and each consonant sound (phoneme) can be heard individually; the term *consonant cluster* refers to the written form, while the term *consonant blend* refers to the spoken form, but many use them interchangeably.

decodable text—texts that contain a large percentage of words that incorporate the letter-sound relationships students have already been taught

digraph—two letters that make one sound; **consonant digraphs** are two consonants together that make a single sound, such as /ch/, /sh/, /ph/, /wh/, and /ck/; **vowel digraphs** are groups of two letters together that make a single sound, one of which must be a vowel

diphthong—a new sound formed by combining two vowels in a single syllable; examples of diphthongs include *ow, ou, aw, au, oi, oy*

Dolch Word List—a list of 220 high-frequency words created by Edward William Dolch in 1936. The list is arranged based on the frequency of use in reading materials of students in kindergarten through second grade and does not contain any nouns. A separate list of 95 high-frequency nouns was later created.

etymology—the study of word origins and how meanings have evolved and changed over time

explicit—stated clearly and in detail; explicit instruction is where skills are taught directly to students through lessons with clear objectives and guided practice with scaffolded support

explicit instruction—skills are taught directly to students through lessons with clear objectives and guided practice with scaffolded support

expression—making your words and speech lively; appropriate fluctuations in pitch, timing, emphasis, and intonation when reading aloud; expression can convey the understanding of meaning

fluency—the ability to read with speed, accuracy, and expression

Fry's Instant Word List—a list of 1,000 high-frequency words compiled by Edward Fry in 1957 and updated in 1980. This list contains all parts of speech, and the words are arranged in order of frequency of occurrence in reading material with about 100 words per grade level.

grapheme—the smallest unit in a writing system; a letter and/or letter combination that represents a phoneme

high-frequency words—words that are most used in the English language

implicit—suggested but not directly expressed or stated; implicit instruction is the exposure of students to ideas and concepts through opportunities for interaction with books and/or other materials

irregular words—words that do not follow common letter-sound correspondences or phonics patterns and are not easily decodable

isolation and manipulation—phoneme *isolation* is the ability to isolate or separate sounds at different positions within a word, such as initial, medial, and final, phoneme *manipulation* is the ability to add, delete, or substitute phonemes in spoken words

morpheme—the smallest unit of meaning that cannot be further divided; the smallest meaningful part of a word; examples of types of morphemes: prefix, suffix, base, root

morphology—the study of words and their parts, how words are formed, and how they relate to other words; morphology includes studying morphemes (the smallest unit of meaning that cannot be further divided); the smallest meaningful part of a word

multisyllabic words—words with more than one syllable

onset—an onset is the part of a syllable that comes before the vowel; an onset can be a consonant or a blend; some syllables do not have an onset

orthographic mapping—the process used to store words into long-term memory; a cognitive task where readers make connections between phonemes (sounds) and graphemes (letters) to combine and recall the pronunciation, meaning, and spelling of words quickly and effortlessly

phoneme—the smallest unit of sound in spoken word, usually characterized by these marks / /; there are 44 phonemes in the English language

phoneme/phonemic awareness—the awareness of the smallest units of sound (phonemes) and the ability to manipulate those sounds

phrasing—grouping words together when reading to sound more like talking instead of reading one word at a time

prefix—a root attached to the beginning of a word; generally, a prefix gives a word direction, negates a word with the meaning "not," or intensifies a word's meaning by adding the notion of "very"

prosody—reading with expression

rhyme—the correspondence of sound between words or the ending of words

rime—the part of a syllable that includes the vowel and any consonants that follow; all syllables have a rime because all syllables have a vowel sound

rote memorization—a method of learning where memorization of the skill, fact, or figure is based on repetition

scope and sequence—an organized curriculum that is designed with systematic and explicit instruction that includes repetition and review

sight words—words that can be read automatically, quickly, and with little effort

speed (reading rate)—the rate at which a person reads printed text; usually calculated by the number of words read per minute

suffix—a root attached to the end of a word; generally, a suffix changes a word's meaning and/or part of speech

systematic—organized and carefully planned; systematic instruction means intentionally sequenced lessons and activities to ensure skill mastery

systematic instruction—intentionally sequenced lessons and activities to ensure skill mastery

trigraph—a single sound that is represented by three letters; examples include *tch*, *air*, *ore*, *ear*, *igh*, *are*

vowel—any of the following five letters in the alphabet: *a, e, i, o, u*; these letters represent vowel sounds made when the air flows freely when making a sound while speaking; a **short vowel** is a vowel sound that has a shorter duration of the sound being made; a **long vowel** is a vowel sound that has a longer duration of the sound being made; sometimes, the letter *y* acts as a vowel in words such as *my* or *fly* or *cry*

Index

f denotes figure